I0236104

Meals and Memoirs II

Recipes and Recollections of African Americans in Tucson, Arizona

Second Edition

Originally published by the

Afro-American Historical and Genealogical Society-Tucson Chapter

Edited by Tani Sanchez, Ph.D.

Brightwater Ventures, LLC. Tucson, Arizona, 2022
P.O. Box 85272, Tucson, Arizona

ISBN 978-0-9983205-6-4
Second Edition
All rights reserved

©Copyright Tani Sanchez 2022
Originally published in 1993 by the Afro (African) American Historical and Genealogical Society –
Tucson Chapter

Cover image of Red Lentil Soup by Sadie Shaw

Preface and Acknowledgments

This newest edition of *Meals and Memoirs* is dedicated to Gloria Smith, the founder of the Afro-American Historical and Genealogical Society (AAHGS)Tucson Chapter. In its heyday, it existed as an intense center for a small core group of Black people excited about African American genealogy, the diaspora, and the impact and legacy of Black people and their communities. They shared stories, created workshops, attended national conventions and sponsored local events. In the early 1990s, they brought speakers to town to celebrate, explore and explain.

Gloria Smith, author, historian, former lecturer, member of the Tucson Chapter of the Links, Inc and many other organizations.

The Tucson Chapter developed as the brainchild of Gloria Smith, a former University of Arizona research librarian, and fellow Tucsonan Richard Harris, who had published an Arizona guidebook. Smith previously served as a founding member of the national AAHGS, personally invited by James "Dent" Walker, director of Local History and Genealogical Programs, and assistant director of the Institute of Genealogical Research at American University. Harris and Smith later met at a genealogy conference and decided that they had to create a Tucson chapter. Smith, originally from Pittsburgh, Pennsylvania., did what she would do many times in the future. In a town with then less than a 4.3 percent Black population, she created Black organizations and events that she wanted to exist. Over the years, she founded a Black book publishing club and the Helen Lott Memorial Ladies Auxiliary of the Buffalo Soldiers. Active in many local social organizations, Smith had already arranged and promoted a Tucson-based Annual Meeting of the formerly all-Black 9th and 10th Cavalry Regiments by 1991. This promotion garnered the support of then Arizona Gov. Rose Mofford and then Sen. John McCain.

 In December 1990, Smith recruited interested locals for the Tucson AAHGS chapter. In the early days, we traveled together to Phoenix to attend the AAHGS Arizona chapter meetings. By December 1991, the Tucson chapter had formed, and held its first annual meeting a year later at the Tucson Hilton East. Perhaps as many as 100 enthusiastic people attended a day full of sessions and presentations. In the following years, the Tucson Chapter met monthly to share research and stories of the Black past and to discuss their own genealogy projects and family history. The group produced a newsletter alternately called Dry Heat or the Desert Griot. Edited by Smith, it featured articles about Arizona. Readers learned about about Holbrook Arizona, the town of Black cowboy Nat Love before he became "Deadwood Dick." Other editions explored stories and research on topics such as the naming of Pinetop, Arizona, said to be the nickname of a Black man who originally came from McNary, Arizona.

The gatherings always included food. Members met in their homes, serving foods dear to their diverse range of African American tastes, such as one evening of memorable Louisiana gumbo. The food represented the complexities of African American cultures. Soon, the group began regularly meeting in the Arizona Historical Society board room. Although the venue changed, food still played a distinct role as the chapter evolved. When annual meetings met in hotels, care was taken to ensure the meals reflected a Black interest. For example, the 2005 "Genealogy and DNA" meeting featured a catfish brunch. On at least two other occasions, Art and Vel's soul food restaurant created meals featuring cassava breads and other items associated with an African influence. The organization shared its Afrocentric meals with the Tucson public by hosting annual events at the Arizona Historical Society.

In 1993 the group began discussing a historical cookbook. As an officer and founding member, I suggested it as a fundraising and interviewing activity. It was never meant to be only a cookbook. All members supported the project. We interviewed the city's oldest residents, taking notes. These people saw and could speak about life in past decades, about changes before and after segregation ended. The focus was Black Tucson history *and* food, married together. As a fundraiser, *Meals and Memoirs* in various versions, sold for at least the next five or so years.

After more than two decades, membership dwindled and the chapter was no longer active. In the early 2000s, I wanted to update the cookbook. People kept asking for copies of the old edition, but none were available. I contacted the officers from the original group and got permission to proceed. I had kept the old manuscripts, and later purchased picture permissions from the Arizona Historical Society, but school requirements, mothering and other obligations prevented me from acting further. In 2020, a University of Arizona Agnese Nelms Haury grant allowed for the hiring of students from Africana Studies to interview and transcribe the thoughts of contemporary community members and to collect their recipes and images. Interviewers included Saydou Bonsa, Janet Morris, and Emani Spencer. Many thanks and acknowledgement to them. The Haury grant included input that influenced the inclusion of various editor's notes about contemporary health concerns. Everything kickstarted from this point despite Covid 19 pandemic delays.

Also, to be thanked are the select members of the local community who donated recipes and consented to be interviewed. New names came from all over, including a committee, my recommendations and other sources. Updating the original project included a small but eclectic group of people from many backgrounds. People who provided some editing content include Dunbar Board of Directors members Chryl Lander as well as Barbara Lewis, long time Tucson residents.

Special thanks also to Jerome Dotson, Ph.D. for his written introduction. A native of Atlanta, Georgia and a graduate of Morehouse College, his research and teaching interests focus on African American history, Southern food ways, hip hop, folklore and politics of the body. Currently, he is working on a book-length manuscript, which explores the ways eating and diet have animated Black radicalism in the 19th and 20th centuries. Recognition similarly goes to other colleagues including Dr. Geta LeSeur-Brown, Dr. Howard Smith, Dr. Bryan Carter and the Dr. Bayo Ijagbemi family who provided recipes, some edits and interviews. Although the pandemic, an illness and other concerns delayed the publication, it is finally here! In this new edition, nutrition notes from various national sources are included.

The Afro-American Historical and Genealogical Society Tucson Chapter is acknowledged as the original publisher of the first edition. Those original chapter members included Gloria Smith, Emily Ricketts, Hearon Hayes, Marguerite Euell Sanchez, Adalina Comeaux, Pecolia Hayes, Pearl Chandler, Effie Gregory, Mona Mouton Blackburn, Dan Summers, Richard Galloway, Charles Spears, Doreen Davis, Etta Dawson, Beverely Elliott and Lorraine White.

This is a book with the original purpose intact—to combine history, biographical snippets, and recipes of a local population. The idea is to put Tucson in a context where there is a bit for everyone. It offers new recipes and new stories alongside the original ones. These living histories encompass concerns such as the COVID-19 pandemic, contemporary health cuisine concerns and just a touch of Black social protests. *Meals and Memoirs II* tells a story of Black people in Arizona still living, influencing, generating, and surviving as they create distinct meals and wonderful stories that all can savor.

Tani Sanchez, Ph.D., editor

Contents

Introduction

by Jerome Dotson, Ph.D.

Meals and Memoirs II is a beautiful cookbook that also offers critical insights into Black Tucson. In many ways, it reminds me of the cookbooks produced by the National Council of Negro Women. Since there are so few histories of Black life here, I think this is an indispensable text for those who want to know what life is like for Black folks in the Old Pueblo.

For many Black Americans in the early 29th century, proper eating was an essential part of being a good citizen. Noted Black leader Booker T. Washington hired Alice J. Kaine, a white home economist from Wisconsin, to transform students' dietary habits at Tuskegee Institute in the 1890s. Eschewing pork for beef, Washington saw beef as an important symbol. Historian Jennifer Jensen Wallach (2015, 168) writes, "It seems likely that his connection with Kaine and other white food reformers encouraged Washington to value beef not only as a nutritious food but also as an instrument of civilization." But the Wizard of Tuskegee was not only promoting class ideals. Pellagra, a disease brought on by malnourishment, was common throughout the South by the early 20th century. Medical experts believed that the prominence of this sickness among many rural Southern whites and Blacks was a by-product of monotonous diets mainly based around pork and corn. Booker T. Washington's efforts to promote more balanced eating also aimed to counter the effects of this pernicious disease.

The National Association of Colored Women, founded in 1896, also promoted better living among Northern Blacks by focusing on health and children's nutrition. Organizing milk programs in the early 1900s, the organization provided milk to young children to combat infant mortality. "Milk programs," writes Susan L. Smith (2010, 24), "were especially needed for Black infants, whose mortality rate was generally higher than that of white infants." During the 1950s, the National Council of Colored Women continued to display an interest in food and nutrition. In 1958 the organization published *The Historical Cookbook of the American Negro*, which aimed to promote modern eating, especially among newly arriving Black migrants from the South. Anne Bower (2007, 159) writes, "Typical of community (or fund-raising) cookbooks, *The Historical Cookbook of the American Negro* is intended for middle-class African Americans, and its compilers sought to maintain certain values of mainstream society, particularly upward mobility and propriety."

In the 1960s and 1970s, Black American health advocates like Alvenia Fulton worked alongside Black physicians to push for healthier eating in response to rising rates of hypertension and diabetes among Black Americans. Fulton promoted "Soul Food with a Mission" and encouraged Black Americans to adopt vegetarianism and intermittent fasting. Similarly, cardiologists like Dr. Elijah Saunders and Dr. James Mays advocated for the adoption of more heart-healthy choices.

From Booker T. Washington to Dr. Alvenia Fulton and Dr. James Mays, Black Americans have had a long tradition of connecting nutrition to longer lives. In a similar vein, the contributors to *Meals and Memoirs II* acknowledge the importance of Black American culinary traditions while fostering healthier visions of long-beloved dishes. By offering recipes as well as stories and interviews from Black Tucson, *Meals and Memoirs II* promises to nourish both the body and the mind.

Life in Tucson, Early Settlers and Many Migrations

On sofa, left to right: Monicia Porter holding her son, Jordan, Monicia's grandparents Gladys and Eugene Huff. Kneeling behind sofa: Stan Porter, Monicia's father David Robins. Back: Monicia's mother Murieljean Robins, son Dale Joyce Jr.

In 1900, records indicate that just 86 people identified themselves as of African descent in Tucson, Arizona. By 1930, a tally came up with 1,003, and in 1990, census records placed the Black population at just over 16,000. Tucson's Black population in 2022 is just over 5 percent of its overall 548,073 residents. Yet this percentage represents a great leap in numbers over past decades when the percentages have been 3 percent or less. A relatively small group, African Americans nonetheless form a distinct part of the fabric of this city. We count and we make a difference in all the ways that black people always have. We have challenged norms, added to the wisdom that comes from differing standpoints, and offered cultural expressions that enrich everyone in multiple ways.

Mr. and Mrs. Matthews, Tucson Arizona residents circa 1910s.

At the beginning was Estevan, a member and scout in a Spanish expedition. In 1526, he traveled to the area that would become Arizona. Local historian Dr. Harry Lawson writes that Estevan "was the front man for an expedition of Spanish explorers under the leadership of Fray Marcos de Niza, Vice Commissioner-General of New Spain, searching for the fabled 'Seven Cities of Gold' or Cibola. This was in 1539...However, there would be a long span between Estevan's arrival in Arizona and the coming of other Blacks — over 300 years."

Two of the first recorded Black settlers in Tucson are Mr. and Mrs. Wiley Box, who arrived between 1850 and 1855. Their occupations included stagecoach driving, manual labor, prospecting, and a bit of everything else. From New Orleans and Oklahoma respectively, the young couple lived out their natural lives in the city. Charley Williams ("Banjo Dick") was another mid-19th-century pioneer. One account says, "old settlers of Tucson cannot help but call back to their memories the beautiful strains played on the banjo by this serenader."

Edmond Robinson, who arrived in the 1890s, also stands out. Formerly a Texas foundry foreman, by 1905, Edmond was running a two-story rooming house in Tucson with his wife. Located next to the old Heidel Hotel facing what was then called Arizona Short Street, the Robinsons' rooming house clientele included African Americans and Asians as well as a German baker and an Irish carpenter. Military men, stationed at Fort Apache and Fort Huachuca, began arriving during the Indian Wars. In those early days of segregation, Black men and women typically worked as cooks, waiters, and miners, although others owned businesses that served their communities. Some homesteaded or worked just outside of Tucson as field hands picking cotton. Black people were not enslaved in Arizona, but some arrivals were sponsored and brought to the state because of labor needs such as cotton harvesting.

In the early 1900s, Black settlers such as the Prestons bought 160 acres near what is now known as the Palo Verde Overpass. Joe Moncrief and Mary Felix are reported owning ranches near the same area. In the wake of renting and selling restrictions, as more Blacks arrived, many settled in the "A" Mountain area, becoming the first non-American Indian residents to build homes there.

As the next century progressed, other African American neighborhoods formed as more Blacks arrived.

One community formed on the southside and by the 1960s, neighborhoods also included the then Black middle-class "Sugar Hill" section between East Grant Road and Speedway Boulevard. Now, as in the past, Black migrations, traditions, and influences vary. Many came because of the military, such as the Porters in the 1920s. The Curley and Mary Euell family first came to northern Arizona arriving from Louisiana in 1924, following the sawmill industry. They moved to Tucson, more than 200 miles south, just a few years later, seeking better educational prospects for their children. The one available school in McNary did not offer classes for Black children beyond the eighth grades, something the larger city offered. Mary in particular also noted that beyond high school, the University of Arizona technically did not exclude Blacks. She determined her children would attend there as well if at all possible. As early as the 1920s, by one recollection, a handful of Black residents had enrolled, with many graduates later returning to teach at the segregated Paul Lawrence Dunbar elementary and junior high school. Decades later, in 1969, the Merle and Yvonne Gathers' family came because of a football scholarship offered by the University of Arizona. The Shaw family similarly arrived, looking for less racism and more opportunity.

The people who came here had a mixture of expertise, dreams, and successes. They met on special occasions. They celebrated everyday life as well. People would gather on porches to talk and enact events, sometimes serious, sometimes in a spirit of fun. Children played and rode bicycles in the streets. Lifelong friends were made in school, and music and dancing served as popular activities. In a society that freely used their talents, creativity, and skills with little return or recognition, Black Tucsonans created and looked for places of opportunity and safety. Throughout the nation, prejudice and discrimination against Blacks influenced living conditions. Blacks here, as elsewhere, noted their conditions and protested in education, policing, and other areas. As early as the 1930s, Black women of Tucson's the NACWC Progressive and Civic Club petitioned for and received a park for black children so they would be able to swim in pools at all times, not just before cleaning. They also opened up a daycare for working families and sponsored

Founding AAHGS Tucson Chapter member Effie Gregory contributed this image, identified as an "A Mountain home built by African Americans in the early 1900s." Effie and her husband John made their home in that neighborhood for many years after they relocated to Tucson from Chicago. She retired from the U.S. Postal Service and was an active force in many community organizations such as the NAACP, the Juneteenth Festival Committee and the A-Mountain Neighborhood Association. She also hosted a radio gospel program and received the Access Tucson 1996 Award for Cablecasting Excellence for her production of "Women of Color."

musical events.   Men joined the Elks Club and similar organizations, with comparable goals, recognizing needs to both cherish and support their communities. In later decades, Black students held protests at Tucson High School. In 1967, youths threw rocks at police cars and buildings after a Black teenager was arrested a few days before. The assessment of the youths was that the arrest was unjust. The National Guard was called out, two additional youths were arrested, and others were detained. Discussions ended with the creation of a jobs program to address Black unemployment, with resources poured into creating a youth center. It is unclear if grievances about police suspicions or wrongful detainment were addressed.

The University of Arizona also had several incidents. It had long practiced exclusions of access within its system, as explained by earlier students, and in this cookbook's memoir by Elgie Batteau, "A Graduate Student from the 1930s Remembers." As early as 1976, students and community leaders met with Dr. Felix Goodwin, assistant to University President John Schaefer, to discuss the creation of a Black Studies Program. Consistent with other educational institutions of the modern Civil Rights Era, the University initiated a program. However, it was not until 1989, following students rallies and protests for a "formal department" along with an African American Student Center that a "major" turning point occurred. These Black student actions prompted a major overhaul that resulted in programs and cultural centers on campus not only for African Americans but for other marginalized groups such as Mexican American and American Indian studies. Local Black civic groups, such as the NAACP, played roles advising and supporting the 1989 efforts. In 2022, the program finally became a department, now with the name of Africana Studies. In 1992, reports of tense relationships between the University Police Department and Black students surfaced, with students alleging harassment and officers refusing to assist Black students. Mandatory cultural sensitivity training was ordered for officers.

In 2007, University of Arizona white students "celebrated" Martin Luther King Jr. Day with a racially themed party. In blackface makeup and wearing do-rags, participants wore fur coats to mimic gangster stereotypes; the event theme was "Favorite Black Person." Organizers insisted it was "harmless fun" but in a later UA forum to discuss the party, Black students expressed their disgust and requested "mandatory classes in diversity and race relations." In 2019, two apparently drunk white students hurled racial epithets as they attacked and beat a Black student. They eventually faced misdemeanor assault charges, but only after angry protests by students. In the Tucson Unified School District, in 2021, a Black high school girl, Ashlee Diggles, began petitioning for an anti-racist curriculum that would be required for all in her school district. The objective was to make mandatory "the requirement of texts with at least one author, in high school English and history classes, from ethnic and racial minorities, as well as lessons on bias awareness and micro-aggressions." Her petition arose from an incident in class that she found insensitive.

The increasingly common visual depictions of national killings and assaults on Black people in the 2020s affected Tucson as well. Cell phone video footage of George Floyd's death in May 2020 sparked local activity as many citizens of all races joined in protests proclaiming that Black Lives Matter. During Juneteenth that year, Tucson Mayor Regina Romero commemorated the holiday by recognizing a Black Lives Matter banner hanging off City Hall. Murals and other artwork appeared in several sites downtown, and Stone Avenue, a street in the heart of Tucson, was painted with the words "Black Lives Matter". Websites promoted information about Tucson resources, and about racial equity and its impact. Members of BLM Tucson in May 2020 hosted "a virtual Black healing event." By June 2020, protestors marched downtown carrying George Floyd signs, posters, and American flags. At the Dunbar Pavilion, hundreds of citizens from all races listened to speeches and local testimonies by people whose family members lost lives through police actions. The event culminated in candle lighting and a moment of silence. The University of Arizona announced counseling services for students traumatized by Floyd's death, and various departments and programs denounced the killing for its "disregard for human life." Pima County Public Library and the Arts Foundation for Tucson and Southern Arizona similarly issued a statement. State legislators asked for various commitments to "dismantling racism and increasing education about how racism affects health, and to support policies to improve health in communities of color."

Interviews About Contemporary Life in Tucson

What stories can you say about Black life in Tucson?

Monicia Porter, *Counselor at Tucson High Magnet School*: I grew up in Tucson. I've been in Tucson since I was a baby. From a baby to 18, well really to 17 … Then I joined the Marine Corps and I was gone for a long while, probably about 30 years. Not quite 30, but I've always gone back and forth. I came home for a couple years and I went to graduate school at the University of Arizona. I came home again for a couple of years, transitioned back, went to Atlanta, Dallas, back to Atlanta, then I went to combat. There's nothing like combat to make you appreciate your family. After combat, I came back home to be closer to my family. I've been back home now for about six years.

Sadie Shaw, *Tucson Unified School District Governing Board member, community activist.* There are still many Black families in Sugar Hills [a historically Black Tucson neighborhood]. We're not like the Dunbar area where maybe it's one percent. There are about 20 percent Black families. Of course, that is nowhere near what we were and what I hope will change in Sugar Hills. Gentrification and all of that has led to the loss of Black homeownership in Sugar Hills. But with the Donna Liggins Center [a city recreation site], Black people still use the neighborhood and of course we have the two Black churches in the neighborhood who are some of the oldest Black congregations in Arizona: Mount Calvary and Mount Olive.

Editor's note: Donna R. Liggins worked for the city of Tucson for almost 40 years; the Donna R. Liggins Recreation Center is named after her. She is highly active in NAACP events, the Black Women's Task Force, the Juneteenth Festival Committee, and other Black organizations.

Anton Russell, *program director at The Drawing Studio, a non-profit arts organization.* My grandparents moved here in 1951. My grandparents settled in what is known as Sugar Hill. That area is now gentrified and our home, which was at 421 East Waverly, has already been levelled and turned into mini-dorms, so a lot of what Toni Morrison said in terms of place is something that is actually in our bodies—we have no place anywhere in America that we can call our own—is a very real thing for me. Because I am here in Tucson, no matter how we thrive, we struggle still to have a place to call our own. Nothing really brought me here because I was born and raised here. Born and raised in Tucson in 1979, so I am a third generation.

Editor's note: Toni Morrison was a writer who won both Nobel and Pulitzer Prizes. Formerly a professor at Princeton University, she was known for many novels, including *Beloved, The Bluest Eye* and *Sula.*

Eric Oum: the Thrive Guide & Men's Outreach Coordinator at the University of Arizona. After being in Tucson for eight years, I've come to realize that this city buzzes with unique diversity and a rich culture. The more you explore this city, the more you learn about its small quirks and niches which make this place truly special. Over the last few years, I've particularly enjoyed discovering the few small Black businesses littered throughout the city. Despite the small population of African Americans in Tucson, the Black community here is hard-working, welcoming, and most importantly resilient. I meet a lot of Black folk at community facilities like sports centers, and different public courts. Sports and exercise are an integral part of our lives and we find joy and pleasure from doing it with other people. I play volleyball, so I spent a lot of my time playing with other community members in local recreation centers and parks. Working in a team forms bonds among people, and they feel connected to one another from there on. I hope they continue to fund and maintain these community recreation centers, because they encourage underprivileged folk to take part in leisure activities.

Debi Chess: former executive Director Dunbar Pavilion. So, I've been in Tucson for 10 years. We moved here from Chicago for my husband to accept a position here. We have since separated and divorced, but when I moved here, I had no concept of Tucson. Tucson wasn't even an idea in my head. I had a friend that at the time, the executive director of the Urban League. He had invited me out—his name was Jonathan Peck—he invited me out to do some consulting work for the Tucson Urban League, but my experience was, I got off the plane, I went to the meeting, I got back on the plane, I went back to Chicago. So, I didn't really experience Tucson until my husband had said "You know, I'm looking at this position." And so, his Board chair said, "Have your wife come out, and we'll host her and everything." So, I came out and the first thing that struck me was there was an art house cinema here at The Loft, and I thought any city that would have an art house cinema—because it's one of my loves, as well as independent film; that was my first job when I moved here, I was the development director of The Loft—is a city I could live in. [Later] I was really frustrated by the lack of seeing Black people. When we moved here, I thought this was such a wonderful opportunity to be involved in a community this size. So, I kind of fell in love with Tucson because I saw the potential of what was here. Not only the potential; things were going on, and it just needed some wind in its sails.

Yeah, that's how I got to Tucson, is through my ex-husband. Ten years. It's lonely; it's very lonely. And I keep using the word frustrating because for people who were born and raised here, they have an ability to adapt to this environment in a way that, it's impressive. But it's hard for us who are so used to being able to go to something as simple as the hair supply store. Here they have one, Waba, and then you have your Sally's or whatever. But, where I'm from, the beauty supply store, you get your jewelry. I don't wear other people's hair, so I don't go for that, but you can get big old chunks of shea butter. You get every outfit you can imagine. The beauty supply store is as big as Macy's and so you come here, and you have Waba and you're like "Oh, ok." It's very small, very limited. There just aren't Black boutiques to go buy clothing. Just all those things that you take for granted almost when you come from a place like Chicago. The food! The diversity of food, all the diversity of Blackness just isn't as visible here. You have to work really, really, really hard to find Blackness in Tucson, and that's why the Dunbar is so important. Some of my frustrations of working there is this lack of understanding.

Editor's note: In addition to working as the Dunbar Pavilion Executive Director, Debi Chess was Director of Development/Community Outreach and Education at the Loft Theater and was a founding member of the Tucson Black Film Club.

John Greenwood, *site supervisor at a behavioral health residential program:* I grew up on the north side. I came to Arizona, and I think in 1973. I was 11 years old and from New York City. My dad was an entertainer. We did a lot of traveling around the world, so I had different exposure to cultures and different ethnicities and skin colors. I found Arizona a little bit shocking.

I love the Western idea. Dad bought land out in the deep rural area of Marana. We were the only Black people out there. It was a desert thing. We had four or five acres. It was Arizona. It was hot, so it was not what we were used to, but we were children. Eighty percent of the time, maybe I felt accepted. Twenty percent of the time where we weren't. It was a real rural kind of country area, you know, very rural and white. We started using firearms and hunting and then got into sports and did well in sports. So those are things that kind of helped me fit in.

By the time I was in junior high, we had moved into northwest Tucson, which is when I went to high school, which I was one of three or four Black people in the whole school. But again, I think being an athlete probably opened doors and opportunities and things, that maybe other people might not have experienced in school. There were only a few Black people. Anyway, I was accepted well. And I got treated very well. A couple times somebody would step out of line and, you know, I put them in their place or your white friends who would jump in and defend me or champion me, whatever you want to say, so I grew up, kind of like, hey, everything's cool. I mean, it was cool for me. I knew there was a difference, though, and I ran into things that, as an older person I can look back and say, that was kind of messed up there. You know, there were things you just didn't notice as a child.

Yvonne Gathers: Licensed Social Worker. Black life in Tucson was different when we arrived in 1969. I think there were people in the community, and he [Yvonne's husband Merle] was in college of course, so our whole social atmosphere was centered around the University of Arizona. And I had never had a problem getting a job in Tucson. I worked for Tucson Gas and Electric for a few years and of course I know that I probably wasn't advanced because of my ethnicity. But life in Tucson has always been very pleasant. It really has. We met some really good people; most of them were from the East Coast, most of them were athletes and they came here to play ball, and we just all kind of grew up together. We had our children here, and we are still friends. Maybe two, three couples may have gotten divorced, but for the most part, we can kind of put hands on everyone we were friends with when we were younger, before children.

Interviews About Life in Tucson in the 1990s and Before

What stories do you remember about early families in Tucson?

Barbara Tucker, *former nurse in the state prison system and mother of two daughters.* "My family, the Betters family, came to Tucson via Eloy to pick cotton in the early 50s—1950 to '55. Just my grandfather and grandmother, then other family members. They, for the most part, were Christians, Pentecostal."

Dr. Tani Sanchez, *Africana Studies professor at the University of Arizona:* My mother, Marguerite Euell Sanchez, said our family came to Arizona in the 1920s in a train carrying African American, Mexican and white sawmill workers to McNary, Arizona. My grandfather, Curley, was a lumberjack who worked for the Cady Lumber company. The school for Black children only went up to seventh or eighth grade but Mary Wright, my grandmother, made a vow that all her children would attend college. So, in 1933, she moved the entire family to Tucson so that the children could graduate from high school and most others attended the University. My grandmother joined Tucson African American organizations and instilled cultural pride in her descendants. She felt one of her greatest achievements was becoming state president of the National Association of Colored Women's Clubs.

Helen Wilkins, *Former Pima County government employee:* I remember Mr. Kino Hall in the 1930s was a rancher and a cowboy. My friend's father. He was the foreman at Mary West's place in the northeast part of town and anything that went on you had to ask Kino. We used to go and ride horses there. We went on without a saddle. When they began to rent to Blacks, we used saddles.

Editor's note: Mary West is likely the white woman described as a "miner" who unified several properties into a mine and working cattle ranch northwest of Tucson in the 1930s. Called the 3-C Ranch (Columbia Cattle Company), it once mined zinc, copper, and silver and hosted gold prospectors. Owned by several different people over the years, the 3-C is now a bed-and-breakfast. The Mr. Kino Hall mentioned by Helen Wilkins is harder to discover. Research for this specific name during the time of her life has not been successful. Helen Wilkins' father was Lawson Johnson from Saline, Kansas. He died in Tucson in 1951.

Dr. Laura Nobles Banks-Reed: *Educator, business owner, civic leader, and member of Alpha Kappa Alpha Sorority, Inc. and Tucson (AZ) Chapter of The Links, Incorporated:* They worked hard and struggled to eke out a living. They loved their children and wanted the best for them educationally and otherwise.

Marguerite Euell Sanchez, *retired Tucson Unified School District librarian and former Holiday Elementary School Teacher and Dunbar school teacher:* There weren't as many single parent families as now. People stayed married.

Constance Smith, *former teacher at John Spring Junior High School and former Sunday school teacher at Prince Chapel African Methodist Church:* There was more authority over children in families by parents.

Editor's note: After formal segregation ended in Arizona in 1951, the all-Black school, the Paul Laurence Dunbar Elementary and Junior High School, was renamed John Spring Junior High School, and was open to neighborhood children. John Spring closed in 1978 as a result of a desegregation lawsuit filed against Tucson Unified School District (TUSD) by Black families. In 1995, The Dunbar Coalition, Inc., purchased the school from TUSD to renovate it into a museum and cultural center. The former school got a new/old name and eventually became The Dunbar Pavilion in recognition of its original African American educational origins.

Part of life in Tucson involves city-wide charity events and fundraisers. Events such as Annual Autism Walks and Resource Fair attract African Americans. The event features "food trucks, entertainment, children's activities" with goals of providing informationBottom row, from left: Darian Thomas Jr., Darian Thomas Sr., and Persephone Thomas. Second row, from left: Mariah Alvarez and Joshua Alvarez. Third row, from left: Tara Reid, Deborah Reid, and Yvonne Gathers. Fourth row, from left: Jerimiah Alvarez, Isaiah Reid-Alvarez, Laterrian Thomas, Becky Thomas, Tamara Alvarez, and Lorraine Hill Richardson.

Recipes: Appetizers and a Bit of This and That

Appetizers, processed snacks and other tempting foods are often high in carbohydrates. These carbohydrates are generally viewed in a negative light, but they are in foods that spark energy, are found in proteins such as nuts and beans, and in sugars, fats, alcohol, and fruits. The American Heart Association recommends that you limit highly processed foods, and focus instead on whole grains and legumes such as black-eyed peas, green beans, and beans and eat more vegetables. Black contemporary Tucson cooks in this and the following sections have found creative ways to do just that. The older recipes still work using the same ingredients. These recipes include occasional notes about updating ingredients. For me, it's fun to see what others are doing.

JOHN GREENWOOD'S TASTY AND NUTRITIOUS BREAKFAST SMOOTHIE
John Greenwood

This smoothie will get your day started off with excellent nutrition and great taste, and is light on the waist.

John Greenwood is the site supervisor at a behavioral health residential program, one that combines an apartment complex and a behavioral health residential facility. He says, "I stay consistent on my detox drinks that I make my own -- Apple Cider Vinegar drinks. I try to eat healthy. In general, I don't go out to fast food very often. I'm not even once a month. I make most of my food at home. I try to stick to your lean meat and vegetables and fruit."

Ingredients:
2 oz blackberries
2 oz blueberries
Two medium-sized leaf of kale
2 oz of pineapple chunks or seedless grapes
¼ of a small lemon
Seven raw almonds
One tablespoons of chia seeds
¾ of a cup of almond milk
¾ of a cup of green tea

Put fruit, kale leaves, lemon wedge, and almonds in a blender or nutrition extractor. Pour in almond milk and green tea. Add chia seeds. Blend for 30–45 seconds to achieve desired consistency.

You can add more or less green tea or almond milk to achieve your desired consistency. You can add a small amount of honey to sweeten to taste.

MARCUS GARVEY BEAN SALAD AND DRESSING
Barbara Lewis

Barbara is a longtime Tucson resident and a Paul Laurence Dunbar School alumna. She currently serves as vice president of the Dunbar Pavilion. She says her recipe "uses black, red, and green colors of the African American flag that the nationalist leader designed." It also incorporates peanut oil, "in keeping with the spirit of the salad, because it was promoted by African American George Washington Carver and because it's a frequently used ingredient in West African cooking."

Ingredients:

1 lb. can snap string beans, washed and drained
2 scallions, diced
1 (15 ounce) can red kidney beans washed & drained
1 (7.5 ounce) black beans washed and drained

1 stalk celery diced
½ medium green bell pepper seeded and diced
Chopped fresh parsley and pimentos for garnish
(Peanut oil and lime juice dressing recipe follows)

Combine the beans and vegetables in a large bowl. Add dressing below and mix well. Garnish with parsley and pimentos.

PEANUT OIL AND LIME JUICE DRESSING
Barbara Lewis

Ingredients:

¼ teaspoon salt
¼ tsp pepper
¼ teaspoon garlic powder
3 tablespoons lime juice

¼ cup peanut oil
1 tsp prepared mustard
1 pinch dried basil
pinch of dried parsley

Put salt, pepper and garlic powder into a mixing jar; add lime juice and shake until seasonings have blended with juice. Add peanut oil, mustard, basil and parsley. Shake again.

Editor's note: Professor Robert Hill identifies Marcus Garvey as a person deeply involved in the design of the Black Pan-African flag. Initially a symbol representing people of the African Diaspora, several Black nations around the world adopted its colors. "Red stood for blood — both the blood shed by Africans who died in their fight for liberation, and the shared blood of the African people. Black represented, well, Black people. And green was a symbol of growth and the natural fertility of Africa." In 1914, the Jamaican born Garvey founded the Universal Negro Improvement Association, inspiring millions to openly respect their roots and consider Black nationalism.

CANDIED PEEL
Marguerite Euell Sanchez

From her childhood growing up in the all-Black section of McNary, Arizona, Marguerite remembered snow-filled Christmases and the American Indians who occasionally walked through the town. One of five siblings, she helped make this brightly colored treat during the holidays with her brothers and sisters in the

1920s. Marguerite taught at the segregated Paul Laurence Dunbar School and School and other Tucson Unified School District schools. She later redirected her career and became a librarian.

Ingredients:

Orange, lemon and grapefruit peels	Food coloring
Sugar to sweeten	Powdered sugar
Water	

Cut orange, grapefruit, and lemon peel into thin strips. Put sliced peels in a small saucepan and add water to cover by about 2 inches. Sweeten with sugar to taste. Place on high heat and bring to a boil, then reduce heat to medium-high and boil for 20 minutes or until tender.

While fruit is boiling, put food coloring into a separate bowls or containers for each fruit and mix to desired shade. When fruit peels are tender, use tongs or a fork to remove them from water and place them in the desired food coloring. Stir as fruit cools until it reaches the desired color. Remove peels from the food coloring and place on waxed paper or a wire rack to cool. When cool, roll each strip gently in powdered sugar until lightly coated. This recipe is good for the holidays also.

Editor's note: Most sweeteners can be replaced with keto substitutes in recipes. Sweeteners such as Swerve are made from erythritol, a sugar alcohol, and are sweet without a bitter aftertaste. Although some people steer clear of artificial sweeteners, seeing them as undesirable, the U.S. Food and Drug Administration says "sugar alcohols are slightly lower in calories than sugar and do not promote tooth decay or cause a sudden increase in blood glucose." If you use artificial sweeteners, consider using products such as Swerve, which also has a confectioners/powdered version. If you prefer natural sweeteners, you can substitute honey for corn syrup, but the taste won't be the same. Honey also has more calories. In recipes, consider brown Swerve instead of brown sugar. The flavor worked well for me.

HONEY'S CRAB DIP WITH FRENCH BREAD BAGUETTE OR CRACKERS
Lorna Ingram

Lorna is an insurance agent and business partner. Also, the Vice President of the Tucson Progressive and Civic Club (National Association of Colored Women's Clubs), she says, her profession is part of her family's master plan. "My husband was in management in the insurance agency which brought us across the country, landing us in Lancaster, Pennsylvania, then in Chicagoland, and then finally here [in Tucson]." Of her recipe and cooking, she says, "They [the ancestors] made everything taste good, just the basics. I wish we all could do that, cook like them, but we can't. And that's why these recipes are so important, because some of those ancestors took those good recipes to their graves. I'm sorry, so I had to just come up with my own, which is my little crab dip. That's where we are. I had an aunt that did a good pound cake, and my dad used to make stuffing with oysters in it. I was calling around the family 'Does anybody have that recipe?' Nope. We did nothing to preserve our legacies, so now we young people are growing up [without them]."

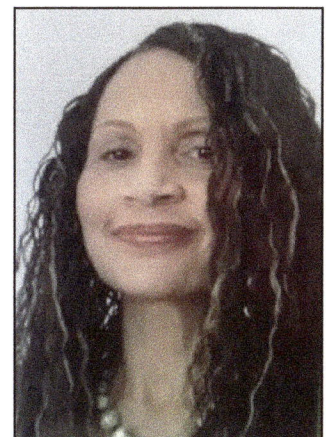

Ingredients:

8 oz. cream cheese

8 oz. sour cream

½ tsp. celery salt

½ tsp garlic powder

1 tsp Old Bay seasoning

¾ lb. Fresh lump crab meat or two (2)- 6 oz. cans premium lump crab meat

Cut baguette into ½-inch thick slices. In a 2-quart saucepan, heat cream cheese and sour cream over medium heat until melted, stirring occasionally. Stir in dry seasonings. Add crab meat. Stir, heat through, and serve immediately over the sliced baguette. Best served at family gatherings and sports parties.

ORGANIC MARGARITA
Tani Sylvester

A pescatarian, Tani prepares most of her own meals, using organic and carefully selected healthy ingredients. She is particular about her choices, and almost never drinks, but that doesn't mean she will not occasionally have some spirits. Raised in Tucson and a frequent visitor home, she is an executive director in the video industry.

Ingredients:

Juice of 1 organic orange

Juice of 2 organic limes

¼ cup organic tequila

1 tablespoon organic simple syrup (natural, no added sugar)

5 organic strawberries

5 handfuls of ice

Mix all ingredients in a blender.

Tani Sylvester says both the tequila and the syrup she uses comes from Whole Foods. The organic syrup is called Dolcedi and is made with apples. The website, www.rigonidiasiago.com/dolcedi/, describes the product as a "natural alternative to traditional sugar." Tani is a graduate of New York University and is a director in a media industry.

COUNTRY CARAMEL CORN
Beverely Elliott

Ingredients:

7½ quarts popped popcorn

2 cups brown sugar

2 to 4 teaspoons baking soda

1½ cups of margarine

½ cup of corn syrup

½ teaspoon salt (optional)

Preheat oven to 200°F.

Place popped corn in a roaster. In a pan, melt margarine over medium-low heat. Add corn syrup, and turn up heat to medium-high. Add brown sugar, stir, and heat through until hot. Sprinkle baking soda into hot syrup mixture and stir to mix. It will become foamy. Remove from heat and pour over popped corn and toss to coat. Bake at 200°F for 45 minutes, stirring every 10 minutes. Remove from oven and cool for 15 minutes. Place in a paper bag. Enjoy.

Editor's note: Beverely Elliott is the executive director and founder of the African American Museum of Southern Arizona. The creative vice president of Elliott Accounting, she was also named the 2007 Tucson's Phenomenal Woman in by the University of Arizona Black Alumni Club.

CAPIROTADA
Hearon Hayes

Hearon and Pecolia Hayes moved to the Navajo Reservation in the Gallup area in 1955, working there for 15 years before returning to Tucson. They had five children. The Hayeses became familiar with many dishes of American Indian and Mexican peoples. According to Fodor's Travels, Capiotada is a Mexican bread pudding with origins in 15th century Spain. It is associated with legends involving Mexican diasporic Jews, ancient Romans, and symbolic Lent and Easter beliefs. North African influences from the Moors "are suspected of helping pave the way for the dessert-like capirotada centuries later."

Ingredients:

2 pounds dark brown sugar

1 cup water, plus extra if needed

2 loaves French bread, sliced

1 to 2 pounds longhorn cheese (Colby cheese), shredded

4 green onions, chopped

1½ pounds walnuts

3 bananas, sliced

Raisins

In a saucepan, add about 1 cup water to brown sugar and heat through until the sugar is dissolved to make a syrup. If the syrup is too thick, add a little more water. Toast French bread till brown. Spread toasted bread on pan. Layer cheese, onions, nuts, bananas, and raisins over the bread, pouring brown sugar syrup between each layer.

PEACH CANTALOUPE PRESERVES
Everlyn Steward Franks

A retired teacher in Tucson Unified School District, Everlyn Stewart Franks moved to the city from Kansas. A civic leader for many years, she was a member of Delta Sigma Theta Sorority, Inc., Tucson Chapter of Links, Inc., NAACP, YWCA, and Delta Kappa Gamma Int. The University of Arizona Black Alumni designated her a "Phenomenal Woman" in 1991.

Ingredients:

2 cups diced cantaloupe

2 cups diced peaches

1½ cups sugar

1 cup corn syrup (for sweeter preserves, increase to 1⅔ cups or to taste)

½ to 1 cup chopped pecans

4 tablespoons lemon juice

1 tablespoon grated orange peel

1¼ teaspoon salt

Cook diced cantaloupe and peaches together in a saucepan for 15–20 minutes. Add sugar. Boil rapidly to thicken. Add remaining ingredients and boil 3 more minutes. Pour into sterilized jars. Put a thin layer of paraffin on top of the preserves.

Editor's note: Artificial sweeteners may not work in home canning.

WEDDINGTON'S BBQ SAUCE
Hearon Hayes

Ingredients:
6 No.10 cans ketchup [114-ounce cans, just over 7 pounds each]

1 quart honey

15 bottles of Worcestershire sauce

2 onions, minced

2 cloves garlic, minced

Garlic pods

Cayenne pepper

Pineapple juice (optional)

Cook onions and garlic well. Add ketchup, Worcestershire sauce, and honey. Use garlic pods [cloves] and cayenne pepper to taste. Pineapple juice may be cooked down to syrup and added.

Editor's note: Low-sugar ketchup is available in most stores if you want to make that substitution. However, the #10 ketchup size can is a large restaurant-kitchen storage size unit ranging from 104-117 fluid ounces and is not typically available in most regular supermarkets, but instead in places like Costco.

BUFFALO WINGS
Tani Sanchez

Ingredients:
Chicken wings

Salt and pepper to taste

1½ stick butter

1 regular (not large) size bottle Louisiana Hot Sauce

Ken's or Wish-Bone Chunky Blue Cheese Dressing

Sprinkle wings with salt and pepper and fry until cooked. Melt butter and mix with hot sauce. Adjust butter and sauce for your taste. Place foil on a cookie sheet. Dip fried chicken into sauce mixture, then arrange on foil. Drizzle chicken with remaining sauce mixture. Broil in oven until crispy and brown, turning if necessary and monitoring constantly. Serve with blue cheese dressing.

Tani Sanchez's family arrived in Arizona in the 1920s. She remembers her grandmother's savory Louisiana cooking, tales of life in the South and stories of ancestors before and after American slavery. She began making these wings after coming back from Army overseas duty in the late 1980s. The wife of a fellow National Guardsman shared this recipe with her during trips to Phoenix.

CHRISTMAS EGGNOG
Hearon Hayes

Ingredients:

2 (3.4 ounce) packages of vanilla pudding and pie mix
1 cup of sugar
1½ gallons milk, divided
6 fresh eggs, separated

1 cup of brandy
1 tablespoon of vanilla
2 cups of fresh-whipped cream
nutmeg

Combine pudding mix, sugar, and 1½ cups of milk in a saucepan. Lightly beat egg yolks and add to saucepan; stir well. Add remaining milk and mix well. Cook over medium heat stirring constantly until mixture comes to a full boil. Cool. Beat egg whites and fold into cooled mixture. Add brandy and vanilla; chill several hours. Add whipped cream and sprinkle nutmeg on top when ready to serve. Should serve 24.

Editor's note: If you use an alternative sweetener in this recipe, try low-sugar alternatives that do not have an aftertaste, such as monk fruit. According to Banner Health, monk fruit has no calories, no sugar or carbs, is not "chemically derived" and "can taste up to 200 times sweeter than standard table sugar." My observation is that indeed it has no aftertaste—an important consideration for me. Banner Health also says "this melon-like fruit, which is oddly closely related to its cousin the cucumber, is picky about where it grows, so it may be why you don't see it in your local produce aisle. The health benefits of monk fruit have long been well-known in traditional Chinese medicine, but its popularity has been growing in the U.S."

SOUTHERN SWEET TEA
Tani Sanchez

Ingredients:

8 cups water, divided
6 tea bags

⅛ to ¼ teaspoon baking soda
1½ to 2 cups sugar

Boil 2 cups water and then remove it from the stove. Place tea bags and baking soda in a deep glass pitcher and pour the boiling water over them. Steep for 15 minutes and then remove the bags—do not squish them. Add sugar to taste and stir until dissolved. Add 6 cups cold water. Let cool in your refrigerator for many hours. Adjust sugar and tea to your taste.

Ingredient Note: You can use a sugar substitute and add lemon slices and mint leaves. Sugar substitutes include monk fruit, powdered Swerve, and stevia. Pick your stevia well if you use it. I have had some that are bitter, but *Stevia in The Raw* and Kroger's stevia work fairly well.

Education, Growing and Learning in the Old Pueblo

University of Arizona Africana Studies' Study-Abroad students in Paris in 2002. Photo used with permission.

Today, most Black students who attend schools in Tucson, of all ages and grades, will be hard pressed to find many other Black faces in their classes. While Black students are present at most local educational institutions, the percentages are extremely small. The Black student enrollment at the University of Arizona stands at roughly 4 percent. At Pima Community College, it is 5 percent, while high school numbers vary from a high of 13 percent to less than 1 percent. In 1970 when Pima Community College opened, 19 total Black faculty taught but that number decreased by 2017. A statement to the PCC Governing Board that same year reports "there are maybe 6 or 9—it depends on which chart—African American faculty at PCC, and about the same number for Native American faculty members. Today, better than 78 percent of the faculty are white at PCC."

This means that seeing another Black face, whether a teacher or student, cannot be taken for granted, and can even seem to be a minor miracle. Cultural theorist bell hooks theorizes that when Blacks in predominantly white environments choose to group together, it is to create safe spaces of refuge. In these safe places, cultural expressions, Black phenotypes, and even Black existences are accepted as ordinary and natural. People are not routinely "othered" and can take time to breathe, to relax without confronting racial biases and marginalization. Black students, parents, and administrators have felt the need to address these types of issues for many years on a recurring basis.

The University of Arizona formally addressed these concerns following 1970s student protests for better academic and social experiences. Local Black organizations such as the Tucson Chapter of the NAACP worked in unison with protesting students. The local post-integration activism fell in line with a larger national Black student push for college experiences that rejected indoctrination, biased teaching, and incomplete or inaccurate histories. As a result, a few Black faculty and administrators were hired and the Black Studies program -- later renamed Africana Studies -- came into existence. Additional protest in 1991 resulted in the creation of African American Student Affairs and a cultural resource center within the Martin Luther King Jr. building on campus. With a mission of providing academic support, leadership development, and cultural events, the center has become a place where "your Blackness is welcome and celebrated!" The Black efforts led to similar accommodations for American Indian and Mexican American university populations. By 2016, "the cultural and resource centers at the University of Arizona campus, banded together and formed the Marginalized Students of the University of Arizona (MSUA). The MSUA made national news as students marched, protested, and created a list of demands to present to the university administration."

Other changes appealed to contemporary Black student life.. In sync with national trends among other Black students on predominantly white campuses, residential dormitory spaces were created that incorporated "Black/African American/African cultural knowledge and experiences with academic support." The B.L.A.C.K. theme hall in Pima Hall has a waiting list and offers "a culturally affirmative living space [where students are engaged] to think about identity—past, present, and future—to help develop their understanding of purpose and mission here at the UA and beyond. Through program-specific activities, group meetings, and workshops, students in B.L.A.C.K. will build an intentional, accountable, and intergenerational community while developing their own leadership potential via outreach initiatives and mentorship." During the COVID-19 pandemic, African American Student Affairs sent informational newsletters to its Listserv while students often communicated via podcasts, Facebook, and online events.

Pima Community College offers students an Ethnic, Gender & Transborder Studies concentration for those interested in complexities of identity. In 2020, the college published a 'Resolution on the death of George Floyd' condemning his murder and committing to "creating a safe and inclusive space for our students and employees of African descent." Inclusion and recognition activities at high schools consist of culture clubs, locally sponsored annual ceremonies with dinners, and scholarships.

Many may be surprised to realize schools were not segregated in the traditional sense during Arizona's territorial and early statehood days. Native American, Mexican American, African American and white children all went to the same institutions. The Academy of St. Joseph, for example, opened in 1867 in Tucson and admitted African American children. Other early integrated schools included Drachman and Davis Elementary schools and Safford Junior High School. Integration was not about perceptions of equality or goodwill efforts; it was a financial expediency. There were not enough Black students to merit the expenses of a separate building. Students were instead shunned and isolated within the classroom, via segregated homerooms and restrictions on activities.

Students and teachers at Paul Laurence Dunbar School, circa 1940.
Photo from Marguerite Euell Sanchez collection.

Segregation laws passed the Arizona legislature in 1909. Tucson's Paul Laurence Dunbar School opened just three years later, and became Tucson's only segregated educational facility. A Mr. Cicero Simmons reportedly taught the first classes, held in a vacant building at 215 E. Sixth Street, next to Stone Cyper's bakery. In protest of its opening, African Americans boycotted the school for two weeks. The Denkins family finally broke the strike. The school had one teacher to teach nine grades and, as the year progressed, about 11 students. The school moved into larger facilities after numerous petitions by parents and community members for equal facilities and increased numbers of teachers.

Once the Paul Laurence Dunbar School opened at the corner of West Second Street and North 11th Avenue, it became the site of many community-oriented events, such as a 1943 Masquerade Ball sponsored by the University "Y" Girls Club. Dunbar was so beloved and nurturing that alumni returned decades later to celebrate their prior beloved interactions at the school.

Students graduating from Dunbar transferred to Tucson High School. As mentioned previously, segregated homerooms and restrictions on school activities were normalized. African American high school students instead participated in Black community sponsored events, clubs and organizations, not receiving much from the segregated public institution. Creation of an all-Black high school was a subject of intense debate and feeling among the African American community but not considered financially practical.

Interviews about Contemporary Education

Sadie Shaw, *Tucson Unified School District Governing Board member, community activist:* We're going to be the minority, whether it's education or jobs. I think Tucson Unified School District is starting to do more and has a long way to go. I think a lot of it has to do with curriculum. African American curriculum and U.S. history. It's unfortunate in 2021 our history is in Black History Month or during those parts of the year where teachers touch base on slavery. I think having TUSD's African American Student Services is key, but of course we have to find a way to make our history a part of the curriculum at all times of the year. I would like to see more of a history of Africa: the culture, the civilizations, and how all of those cultural traits have carried on with Africans in the diaspora. And the knowledge itself is critical to helping Black students do better in school, because I think it's psychological warfare how if the only thing you learn about is how our ancestors were enslaved. It gets into your psyche that they internalize that. I think there is no emphasis on Africans pre-slavery.

Dr. Bryan Carter, *Africana Studies professor at the University of Arizona who teaches Study-Abroad students who travel to Paris to learn of notable expatriates, such as James Baldwin* For many Black students, they unfortunately don't really have "study abroad" in their realm of thinking when they come to University of Arizona. Most don't consider they can afford it. But what it does is it broadens their perspectives. It gives them a sense of not only the world but also the place of people of African descent in other parts of the world, and it gives them a different perspective of how people in other parts of the world thinks about America. So, I love to expose students to other places, to other cultures, and really give them a sense that the world is much bigger than wherever they have traveled to in the past. They can't believe that they are in that place. They've always heard about it, seen it in movies. They wonder over the architecture. Some have been in tears when they first saw the Eiffel Tower. I've seen that so many times. I know that's transformational. I also know that many also feel that many in their communities never thought that they would be able to travel abroad, travel with many athletes. People in their communities were giving them money because they were so proud of them for being able to go other places; they wish they could go. Sometimes those same students continue on as majors and minors in Africana Studies because this has piqued their interest. They see themselves in a bigger picture of people of African American descent having very similar experiences. And not only do we study about that in the classroom, but when we go to some of the ethnic neighborhoods in little Paris or when we go to little Africa or any of the restaurants and they hear some of the same stories, they see some similar situations, they know that the commonalities between our collective experiences of people of African descent are greater than they are less similar.

Petra Robertson, *Published writer and administrative professional:* Most of my experience has been at the university. I'm a volunteer; I always volunteered with AASA [African American Student Affairs], and any time there were any programs the Africana Studies program had, I was a supporter. I am also a supporter financially. I try to be an advocate for students, because when I was a student, I was one of the older students. A lot of times, I would hear them say "Oh, I can't believe that happened," or something like that and me being the person that I would tell them, "Well, you know, I was born in the '60s, so yeah, it did happen," you know? They would be fascinated because it's hard to believe all the stuff that they're hearing. So, being an advocate for students means I can share my experience and let them know, yes, it is true. So, that's one of the things I enjoy doing.

Monicia Porter, *Counselor at Tucson High Magnet School:* I love what I do. My grandmother told me when I was 19, I should be a teacher or social worker and I was like "They don't make any money. I'm not gonna do any of that!" And here I've come full circle when I was 35 and finally entered education. I won't ever look back. I mean I have an opportunity to go back to the corporate world all the time, but I choose to be here. Especially with the peanuts they pay here in Arizona. Come on now! I have to love it.

Anonymous 2021: I am not sure if there can be one "important consideration for the educational success of Black students." A host of factors must come into play to assure the success of Black students. Are we talking about success in higher education? High school? Et cetera. The factors are vast depending on the social background of the students. A kid with a home in the Foothills {affluent areas} will have different experiences from a kid in South Park {lower income neighborhoods}. Nonetheless, family support and intervention at all levels are important considerations for student educational success. In addition to these, discipline and personal drive should be paramount in the student's response to academic work.

Brena Andrews, *Instructional Designer with the College of Veterinary Medicine at the University of Arizona.* I have definitely seen a few try to engage in Greek life—that's the main go-to as far as to feel a connectiveness. Greek life, Black girls' fitness club. I don't really know about organizations. I know there's the Young Urban League; some people who are more about soft politics really like being a part of them. Other than that, I don't really know about any other Black groups, and I think that's why I was so drawn to wanting to start an exclusive Black club at the U of A. Because as you know, something like BSU and any other open club at AASA is open to any student and it doesn't feel exclusive. It's so inclusive and its sort of open and broad that it doesn't really draw enough people for it to feel close or like you're connected to your culture. That's why I wanted to see something like, OK, this is for Black girls and we are connecting because of the fact that we are Black girls and go places and we feel empowered as Black girls. And so, there's not many organizations like that. So hopefully there's more people who try to curate these spaces and create these groups where Black people can feel like they are a part of something that's exclusively for them.

Interviews about Education in the 1990s and Before

What differences have there been since you and your family members attended school?

Dr. Laura Nobles Banks-Reed, *Educator, business owner, civic leader, and member of Alpha Kappa Alpha Sorority, Inc.:* went to an all-Black school. Presently, students attend integrated neighborhood schools. I was used to having old and used school furniture in the classroom. Not so now. I had all-Black teachers. Not so now.

Blanche Lucille Lewis, *Former educator*: The high schools have hired more Blacks in different capacities. Since the integration, the Blacks have been placed all over town. They can attend school in all locations.

Mona Mouton Blackburn, *Former counselor with TUSD African American Studies Program and real estate agent:* Dunbar was Wonderful! Wonderful! Wonderful!

Constance Smith, former teacher at John Spring Jr. High: No more separate schools, separate buses, swimming pools, and dance halls.

Marguerite Euell Sanchez, *Librarian and former teacher at Dunbar:* Integration. Teachers of the Black Dunbar school were sent to other schools, mostly west and south side schools. Teachers are not as concerned with Black students as they formerly were.

Everlyn Steward Franks, *Educator and civic leader, member of Delta Sigma Theta Sorority, Inc., Tucson (AZ) Chapter of the Links, Incorporated, the NAACP, the YWCA, and Delta Kappa Gamma Society International:* Children were more respectful of authority in the past. Parents would investigate and stand by the school. Children knew not to get in trouble at school or they'd get in trouble at home.

Memories of Tucson High School Before Official Integration

Portions of an interview with Catherine White Mize by Marguerite Euell Sanchez

In Tucson High School, we the Black students, were seated in the balcony for all affairs in the auditorium. There was one boy who threw spitballs down the balcony. We had a separate homeroom for only Black students. We also were not permitted to sing in regular group chorus, so the Roberson Glee Club was formed of all Black students. We were not permitted to ride the school buses provided for kids to ride in that lived far from high school. We had to walk.

A Graduate Student from the 1930s Remembers

From an interview with Elgie and Matthew "Mack" Batteau by Adalina Comeaux

Elgie attended the University of Arizona from 1932–1934, completing her master's degree in two years rather than three. She remembers their friend, Dricks, wanted to change his summer registration, but it was lunchtime so they decided to get a soda, a Coke, "at the lunch counter, then in the basement of the Women's gym." They sat and sat and sat, waiting and wondering whether the staff "were going to wait on them."

It was almost time to start registration so they asked for a Coke. The Black waiter went into the back and had some man come out who told them the Coke was $7.59. They said they would take it, but the price kept going up $10 to $20. When they still agreed to pay, he finally said he couldn't serve them.

"Why?" they asked.

"Not my counter, as I just work here" he said, adding that he worked for the alumni. Elgie finally said, "Then you work for me as I am a lifetime member of the alumni."

Two white girls who had heard what was going on came over and said, "Come on. We will go with you and tell them (the alumni) about the incident as he is working for us too." The dean of summer school said it wouldn't happen again.

There was a swimming incident, too. "I could swim as a youngster growing up, but I wanted to take it at the U of A but sessions were always 'full.'" Finally, Ms. Hefney, the instructor, said that her session was full but that she would take Elgie and work with her. After all the other students left, Ms. Hefney would always spend an extra 15 minutes with Elgie teaching her all the strokes. After 5 weeks they were tested, and had to swim 25 laps. Elgie was the first one to complete the task, but did not get a high grade. Later she heard that teachers were told Black students were not to receive an "A" in any class regardless of how good they were. Elgie's English teacher said Elgie read, wrote reports and expressed ideas like the teacher. Elgie was her prized student; but the teacher gave her a "C" because she told her she was not allowed to give high grades to Black students.

Editor's note: The price of Coke was five cents during this time!

Recipes: Nutritious, Fresh Vegetables that Help Us Grow

RED LENTIL SOUP
Sadie Shaw
Serves 4.

Sadie Shaw is the second African American elected to the Tucson Unified School Board. She is an artist and a University of Arizona alumna, and is a member of the Diversity, Equity and Inclusion Committees of both the Arts Foundation for Tucson and Southern Arizona and the League of Women Voters of Greater Tucson. She is also the education program co-chair for the League. She has served as the president of the historically African American Sugar Hill Neighborhood Association. Her family has a legacy of community activism.

Ingredients:

3 tablespoons coconut oil *or* butter *or* olive oil, divided
8 stalks of celery, chopped
1 white onion, chopped
1 whole head of garlic, peeled and chopped
A dash of salt and pepper
2 tablespoons curry powder

2 cups of red lentils
Sliced or chopped vegetables, such as carrots or kale
1 large piece of ginger, peeled
4 to 6 cups or more of stock (vegetable or other)
Cilantro for garnish

Heat a large soup pot on medium-low heat. Add 2 tablespoons of the oil. Add chopped celery, onion and garlic with salt and pepper, then sauté until soft. Add another tablespoon of oil, then stir in curry powder, making sure it doesn't burn. If mixture looks too dry add more oil. Add 2 cups of washed lentils. Mix them in so they absorb the spices. Make sure to add more oil if needed.

Add stock depending on how thick you want it. I start with 5 cups. The lentils need at least 2 cups of stock per cup. Bring to a boil and add sliced carrots. Add a large piece of ginger. Cook until lentils are the desired consistency—from 5 to 20 minutes (whole lentils will take longer than split).

You can add anything to this soup, depending on your preference. If I have kale on hand, I'll put it in the pot 10 minutes before I serve it. I also add cilantro as a garnish if available. Serve with crusty bread, tortillas, or whatever is available.

GROUNDNUT SOUP (GHANA)
Anonymous 2021

Groundnut soup (also known as peanut butter soup) is a popular Ghanaian soup that can be served alone as a meal (depending on the preparation), but is commonly served with other foods (e.g., pounded yam or rice balls, etc.). In Ghana, the groundnut paste/butter which forms the base of the soup is made from scratch. First, the raw groundnuts are roasted and then ground over with a heavy stone pestle (these days blenders are used to turn the nuts into the paste). The Food Conspiracy Co-op on Fourth Avenue in Tucson, Arizona, makes its peanut butter paste through this method.

How much groundnut soup one makes depends on the number of people invited to a meal. Size of cooking pots and saucepans for making groundnut soup can vary from 60 ounces pots to 1 gallon. Most homes in Ghana prefer to add meat, fish, or other seafood. The soup can be made vegetarian and vegan too. That means it can be prepared without any meat, fish, or other ingredients that are not suited for vegan and vegetarian diets. Use of spices such as cayenne pepper, curry, clove powder, cumin, and ginger paste depend on personal taste.

Ingredients:

Groundnut paste
Ginger paste (optional)
Tomato paste (optional)
Meat, fish, or other seafood (optional)

Spices, such as cayenne pepper, curry, ground cloves, cumin
Sliced vegetables, such as onions, garlic, garden eggs, spinach, mushrooms, okra, green beans, cabbage

Fill a pot or saucepan halfway with water and warm over low heat, until it is warm but not uncomfortably hot. Add groundnut paste into the warm water. How much paste one adds depends on the size of the pot and how much soup one wants to make. Slowly use your hands to press and squeeze the paste until it is completely dissolved.

Add a bit of heat on the pot, then add your meat (if using), cayenne pepper, ginger paste, tomato paste, sliced onions, mushrooms, or any choice of other vegetables. Cook for 10 minutes, then add any other spice you wish—salt, for example. Increase the heat and bring the pot to boil. Let it boil for 40 minutes or more. When the soup is done, an oily film will rise and spread over the surface. Depending on how much meat one uses, one can eat the soup as a meal (the groundnut is a good source of protein). However, traditionally, the soup is eaten with rice, rice balls, pounded yam/plantain, etc.

Contributor's note: I have seen this preparation done with the peanut butter sold in grocery stores like Fry's or Walmart. Unfortunately, for some reason these offerings have a very different taste. I do not know why. The best pastes are the organic types made with fresh roasted nuts found in the Food Conspiracy Co-op at 412 N. Fourth Ave. in Tucson.

Editor's note: Garden eggs are described as "Garden egg is a type of eggplant that is used as a food crop in several countries in Africa. It is a small, white fruit with a teardrop or roundish shape that is valued for its bitterness."

FRIED GREEN TOMATOES
Debi Chess

Ingredients:
1 egg
½ cup buttermilk
½ cup cornmeal
4 tablespoons flour (I like to use Wondra)
1 teaspoon seasoned salt (I prefer Lawry's)
½ teaspoon pepper
3 green tomatoes, sliced about ⅓" thick
safflower or peanut oil for frying

Debi Chess

Mix egg and buttermilk and put it to the side. Mix all of the dry ingredients in a shallow bowl or plate. Heat oil over medium heat in a cast-iron skillet. Do not get oil too hot. If oil is smoky, it's too hot. Be sure your pan is large enough to fry 4 to 6 slices at a time; you do not want to crowd the slices in the pan.

Working one slice at a time, dip tomato slices in the buttermilk/egg mixture, then dredge in cornmeal mixture. Place slices in hot oil and fry until golden brown on both sides. Place fried slices on paper towel to drain excess oil, sprinkle with a little more salt and/or pepper to taste and serve. I also eat mine with Tabasco sauce!

This is a family recipe. She says, "When I make fried green tomatoes, I definitely channel my ancestors. I channel my grandmother in her garden. I have a very clear image in my head of the woman I think I am when I'm making fried green tomatoes. It is healthier because of an emphasis on cooking with lighter oils, cooking more with safflower if I decide to fry something. So definitely yes, I am cooking differently and I also look at how the women in my family have aged and how they've managed their health. Some haven't done it as well as they could and I know it's particularly around our diets."

CECIL RICKS' COOKED YAMS
Mrs. Lucille Ricks

This recipe is from Mrs. Hutaker E. Ricks, mother of Buffalo soldier Cecil Ricks, and was submitted by Lucille Ricks, Cecil's wife. Cecil was in the Army for 30 years and was a member of the 10th Cavalry band stationed at Fort Huachuca by 1926. When the band dissolved, he went into the 24th Infantry and eventually spent 17 years at Fort Huachuca. He died in 1976 and is buried at the post. Cecil's favorite dish was cooked yams. He loved these and would eat them any time of the day.

Ingredients:
Yams
Maple syrup
3 to 4 tablespoons butter

Peel yams and slice lengthwise into thick slices. Place in a saucepan and cover with water. Simmer until barely fork tender. Drain. Cover with maple syrup and butter. Cook slowly until yams are tender. You can add English walnuts or Maraschino cherries during holidays.

POT OF GREENS
Mrs. Lucille Ricks

Ingredients:
Greens, such as kale, collard, mustard turnips, lamb quarters, or young dandelions, torn into bite-sized pieces, and washed
Salt pork, cut into 1″ pieces, *or* 2 large smoked ham hocks
Water
Drippings from 2 to 3 bacon slices
1 large red onion, chopped medium fine
2 or 3 garlic cloves, peeled and chopped

Place greens in large pot (about the size of a tub you bathe children in). Add salt pork or ham hocks, drippings, onion, and garlic. Bring to a boil, cover, and simmer 4–5 hours. Stir and add water (that will later become pot likker). Serve with warm cornbread.

FRIED STEAMED CABBAGE
Marguerite Euell Sanchez

Marguerite Euell Sanchez, circa 1940s.

Ingredients:

1 large cabbage, shredded	4 cloves of garlic, peeled and diced
1 cup green onions, diced	1 large bell pepper, diced
	¼ cup of oil
	salt and pepper to taste

Place all ingredients in a heavy pot or skillet and cover. Cook on medium heat, stirring occasionally for 30 minutes. Reduce heat to low and simmer for 15 minutes. Optional: Add hot red pepper flakes and/or sausages.

OKRA, CORN, TOMATO SUCCOTASH
Dr. Laura Nobles Banks-Reed:

Ingredients:

3 tablespoons oil	1 teaspoon pepper
3 cups of fresh or frozen sliced okra	Dash of onion and garlic salts
1 medium onion, chopped	1½ cans (14.5 oz) whole tomatoes, chopped
½ medium green bell pepper, chopped	2 cups of corn niblets
1 teaspoon salt	2 fresh green onions

Heat oil in skillet. Add okra, onion, bell pepper, corn, and seasoning and cook dry for about 15 minutes. Add chopped whole tomatoes to okra. Cover and simmer for 15–20 minutes. Serve over steamed rice and sprinkle with green onions. Enjoy.

POT LIKKER
Morgan Maxwell, Jr.

The son of Dunbar's School Principal Morgan Maxwell Sr., Maxwell Jr. became a celebrated football player at Tucson High School, gained a master's degree and eventually became a real estate residential appraiser. His accomplishments are many and are remembered proudly by the Tucson High Badger Foundation, which recalls that he "was appointed to the post of Deputy State Treasurer by Charles Garland, Arizona's first Republican State Treasurer. He was the first Black in Arizona to become a designated and approved fee appraiser for both the Veterans Administration and Federal Housing Administration. He served as Chairman of the State of Arizona Civil Right Commission."

Ingredients:
4 bunches greens (Swiss chard, turnips, mustard, radish or beet tops)
3 quarts cold water
½ pound salt pork, cut in strips

Put salt pork in a saucepan, cover with cold water, and boil for 45 minutes. Wash young greens in several water changes to clean well. Put into the pot with salt pork and let boil for one hour. Drain the water and season well with salt and pepper. This makes 4 servings.

Editor's note: Morgan Maxwell Sr. was an early principal at the segregated Dunbar School. He was instrumental in naming Estevan Park, a segregated facility built in the 1930s after the Women's Progressive and Civic Club, a Tucson affiliate of The National Association of Colored Women Clubs agitated for a facility where Black residents could freely meet without restrictions or exclusion from public facilities. By 1936, club member Mrs. David had presented Mayor Jaastad with an official request for a park. According to Tucson historian Gloria Smith, Maxwell "decided on the name because Estevan was tied to the Mexicans, Blacks and Whites. The name seemed to fit with all the communities." As mentioned earlier, African explorer, Estevan became the first non-American Indian to enter into what would become Arizona. Estevan Park is located near the Dunbar site and was formerly part of a Yaqui community.

SPICY SQUASH
Marguerite Euell Sanchez

Ingredients:

3 to 4 zucchini squash
¼ cup diced onion
1 clove garlic, diced
margarine
1 small can of whole kernel corn
1 cup of stewed tomatoes

1 cup tomato sauce
1 tablespoon oregano
½ teaspoon red pepper flakes
1 cup grated cheese
bacon bits (optional)

Dice zucchini. Sauté diced onions and garlic in margarine. Add corn, stewed tomatoes, and tomato sauce. Season with oregano and red pepper flakes. Stir most of the grated cheese into the mixture. Transfer to a baking dish and sprinkle remaining cheese and bacon bits on top. Bake for 15 minutes.

Editor's note: The American Cancer Society warns that higher levels of cancer are associated with consumption of bacon and other processed meats. The Cleveland Clinic recommends it be used sparingly and with conditions. Additionally, dietitian Ryanne Lachman, RDN, LD, explains that consumers should "consider serving it alongside a natural dose of vitamin C found in citrus fruits, bell peppers, broccoli, and more. This vitamin C can block formation of carcinogenic substances during those very occasional indulgences." This zucchini recipe fits those guidelines with a 58 percent daily recommended intake of vitamin C.

OKRA-CORN-TOMATOES
Elgie and Matthew "Mack" Batteau

The Batteaus arrived in Tucson in the 1930s. Matthew and Elgie were both educators in Tucson and in Phoenix for many years. Matthew was also an Army veteran. Elgie earned her master's degree, then taught at segregated schools. She was instrumental in renaming the first Black high school in Phoenix, originally called West High, to George Washington Carver High. Elgie later became the first African American to serve on the Pima Community College Governing Board.

Ingredients:

Okra, whole
Oil for cooking
Onions
Garlic

Bell peppers
Red or green chilis
1 can white kernel corn
Tomato juice (optional)

Cut okra into rounds ½″ thick. Cook in oil to rid slime. Chop onions, garlic, peppers, and chilies while cooking okra, adding each to the pan as you finish chopping. Stir often to prevent sticking. Add corn. Add tomato juice if the mixture is too bulky or is sticking. Let cook until done. Serve over rice.

Editor's note: The Batteaus did not provide ingredient amounts, so use your own preferences with this one.

BLACK-EYED PEAS CREOLE
Morgan Maxwell, Jr.

Ingredients:

2 strips of bacon
1 cup onion, chopped
1 cup bell pepper, chopped
1 cup celery, chopped
2 packages (10 ounces) frozen black-eyed peas
1 can (20 ounces) tomatoes

1 tablespoon sugar
1 teaspoon dry mustard
½ teaspoon basil
1 large bay leaf
salt and pepper to taste
Water as needed

Fry bacon until crisp. Remove from fat and drain. Brown onion, green pepper, and celery in fat. Add crumbled bacon. Simmer 5 minutes. Add frozen peas, tomatoes, sugar and seasonings to mixture. Cook slowly for 1 ½ to 2 hours, adding water when needed.

SPANISH CABBAGE
Catherine White Mize

Catherine was a good friend of my mother's. I remember that she informed me of many events in early Tucson when I was writing a report for a graduate class about Tucson recreational events for Blacks before integration. She went to high school here and had many friends.

Ingredients:

1 large cabbage
½ pound salt pork
2 onions, chopped
2 medium white potatoes, chopped
1 bell pepper, chopped
1 can cream corn, about 15 ounces

1 can okra, about 15 ounces
1 teaspoon chili powder
1 teaspoon salt
½ teaspoon pepper
2 tablespoons cornmeal

Cut salt pork in squares, brown in skillet. Add all other ingredients except cornmeal. Simmer about 20 minutes. Sprinkle cornmeal over mixture. Cover and simmer 10 minutes longer.

Religion, Enduring Strength

Pastor Merle Gathers of Christ Kingdom Fellowship Church delivers a sermon for Easter Sunday in 2021, during a Zoom service. Below left, the service featured an Easter play presented by Becky Thomas, Joe Tolliver, and Tara Reid. Below right, Zoom congregants on the top row, from left are: Tara Reid, Tani Sanchez, Yvonne Gathers, and Joe and Marlene White. Second row, from left are: Marilyn Hill, Dolores Townsend, Charlie and Danny Fox, and Chyrl Hill Lander. Third row, from left is Lorraine Hill Richardson, and Deborah Reid is on the fourth row.

Black churches stayed active during the 2020–2021 COVID-19 pandemic. They offered online services and community outreach. Located on Tucson's south side, Rising Star Baptist Church also hosted live Sunday services with masked participants, while simultaneously streaming sermons. The church, with its hundreds of members, also maintained a "Virtual E-Campus," a singles ministry, cell group lessons, and a youth church, all on Zoom. Bible study was still held in the sanctuary. Rising Star also participated in mobile Covid 19 vaccination clinics with at hundreds of community people getting Moderna shots.

Friendship Missionary Baptist Church, located in the Dunbar school neighborhood, had virtual worship on both Facebook and YouTube with members able to comment as the sermons were in progress. During their communions, people were able to follow the stream and use elements of bread and "wine" from their own houses.

Mount Calvary Missionary Baptist Church streamed services from its Sugar Hill location, but this was nothing new for the large congregation. Its television services had long been on Facebook and a Vimeo livestream. During the pandemic, physically distanced members had the option of in-person musical worship, live announcements and a live sermon. Flu shots, a living will workshop, and drive-by mobile food giveaways were part of ongoing ministries.

The non-denominational Christ Kingdom Fellowship, located in the historically Black "A" Mountain area, moved its Sunday services and Bible studies completely online as the pandemic was in full swing—at the strong preferences of its members. Using a Zoom format, the events were nonetheless personal and spirited, with mixtures of live church ministerial attendance, Zoom interactions and prerecorded sermons. Ministerial staff offered communion online while members used a pause in the live Zoom portion to get juice and breads to break, with each participant able to see others as they came and went and as they raise their cups. After the services, the small congregation and the pastoral staff informally shared stories, commented on the message, offered inspirational observations, or asked questions. These interactive Zoom church Zoom sessions were sometimes more prolonged than the prerecorded sermon.

In an innovative move, one Christ Kingdom Fellowship member celebrated a birthday by arranging for a local bakery to prepare special prepaid cupcakes for the entire congregation. Members were asked to pick them up to eat later, but when the announcement was made, younger members offered to pick up the baked goods for older members and deliver them directly to their homes. Pastor Merle Gathers called the Christ Kingdom online services distinctive, and said, "We were able to talk and keep going. That's the unique thing. Nobody's rushing to get off after the sermon." He believes the spirituality of the meetings "has been enhanced. I can see by the questions asked afterwards. We are small and we are all one."

Although virtually all members of Christ Kingdom Fellowship had been vaccinated against COVID-19 by April 2021, plans for returning to their building were delayed as the pastor waited for vaccinations requirements to change and for a few remaining members to vaccinate. In-church services resumed in August 2021 but the congregation kept the online Zoom portion available for members who were not ready to resume in-person worship.

Although still spiritual, these mixtures of remote interaction are a far cry from Black services even just a few years ago. Typically, people were very much in the buildings, hugging, participating in potlucks and in-person choirs.

Horses and buggies, rented carryalls, or hacks brought some African Americans of the 1890s to San Xavier del Bac Mission for Sunday worship services, says one early resident who recalls family tales. Mexican Americans and American Indians were also in attendance. Others attended all-Black Protestant services held in private homes.

In 1943, the Mount Cavalry Missionary Baptist Church Singers, the Singing Carlettes, performed at KTUC Radio Studios.

By the first few years of the 1900s, Mount Calvary Missionary Baptist Church and Prince Chapel African Methodist Episcopal Church had opened their doors, becoming the two oldest African American churches in Tucson. They were followed by the Holiness Church (Church of God in Christ), and Phillips Chapel Colored Methodist Episcopal Church. As centers of religious, self-help, and social activities, they initiated traditional and new auxiliary groups such as the Willing Workers and the Eureka Club.

Churches were entwined with social life. Funding events such as "Heaven and Hell parties" proved to be a huge success. Carloads of church members and friends would pay a fee, and on a set evening would begin visits to designated houses. The "Heaven" homes offered cold drinks and desserts. The "Hell" stops served up hot soups and chili. Boy and Girl Scout troops also met in churches. Dr. Howard Smith, a former Tucson resident and University of Arizona graduate, recalls stories by an older attendant at a Hell party. The hostess received guests in a red dress with a

This is an image I took of Prince Chapel African Methodist Episcopal Church many years ago. Some older members of the A.M.E. church said it is the oldest Black church in the city, but some Mount Calvary histories dispute that.

split up the side!

Box lunches stood out as popular in the early 1900s, with young men bidding for meals prepared by their favored young women. During summer months, daytime services switched to evenings, allowing members to catch the cooler breezes.

Tucson's small African American Catholic population could and did attend churches everywhere, but one, Blessed Martin, was known for its African American ministry. One early attendee took pride in the "colorblindness" of services, saying that although social opportunities were limited, whites, American Indians and Mexican Americans also came to Blessed Martin. Another woman says that after Mass, her aunt and mother would go to the Baptist church so that they could meet and know other members of their race.

Interviews about Religious Life in Tucson from Black Residents of the 2020s

What was the most important aspect of religious life for African Americans in Tucson?

Anton Russell, *Program director at The Drawing Studio, a nonprofit arts organization:* That would definitely be the Black church in Tucson. The Black church has been the community center. And in Tucson, it's meaningful to point out the fact that because of everything we've been talking about with gentrification and exclusion of Black folks and all the places—including the place where you are at the U of A—the places that were not exclusionary and have always accepted people to come as they are, the only things that really are left is barbershops and Black churches. It's the connective tissue for sure, but people are there for their community. You get that from the amount of time people spend after church connected with each other, hugging each other, checking in with each other, and all the extra church meetings and all the extra this and that socialization that comes along with it. As the elders progressed, they found that was their safe space and a time when it wasn't defined as that like we've done in 2020. But that's not for me to find my spiritual center. I find that in myself. I find that at my altar, you know, in my bath water and my cooking, in my spiritual interactions with ancestors, with the universe, or with the earth. When I'm working in the earth, that's, if you want to call it something like a religion, in terms of it being like a spiritual practice. For me, that's where I find it.

Brenda Edmontson, *Business owner, consultant:* Religious life, I don't believe it's different from any other race. You walk the walk. In my case, I'm a Christian, I walk the walk, or I try to walk the walk the best I can. That's it. That's the most important thing, because just like the Bible says, you look at yourself in the mirror and then you turn around and forget who you are and you go do your own thing. That's not walking the Christian walk. That's like people that only go to church on Easter Sunday and the rest of the year you know they're doing their own thing. To me the most important aspect is if you are a Christian, or whatever religion you espouse, that you need to walk the walk. That is the most important thing.

Gloria Smith, *author, historian, former lecturer, member of the Tucson Chapter of the Links, Inc. and many other organizations:* I think we're spending more time together nowadays, learning about each other. Even though we don't have Brotherhood Week anymore, we are still trying to learn about each other and have mutual respect—mutual respect for other religions: Islam, Buddhism, Jainism, which is a very ancient religion. There's a lot of religions we need to learn about. When we were brought in as slaves, we were brought in by Christians, and Christianized, but some people used to sneak off and pray to their own gods. You used to have some beliefs considered as ignorant, but now we look at them and we don't denigrate them the way they were denigrated because we were being enslaved mentally. Therefore, we're having more appreciation for other religions, other ethnic groups.

Editor's note: In the late 1920s, the National Coalition of Christians and Jews created Brotherhood Day as a response to anti-Catholic sentiment. Aimed at promoting religious acceptance, it expanded to Brotherhood Week and remained popular for decades. The conference later renamed itself the National Conference for Community and Justice. According to the organization's Mission page, it "promotes inclusion and acceptance by providing education and advocacy while building communities that are respectful and just for all."

Edria Johnson, *Retired from American Airlines:* I look at Rising Star Baptist Church, how they collaborated with Pima County Health to do the [COVID-19 vaccination] shots. Mount Calvary did it also. Rising Star had over 800 people the first time. And I'm not even a member. I go to Rising Star when I want to go to church, so I am not saying my church was the best church. I was highly impressed. They moved people with these shots through with more professionalism than I have seen in a whole lot of things. The last time the computer broke down. It wasn't as smooth as the first time, but guess what? There was about 600 people there the second time, and by 12 o'clock they all went through. People are going to complain, but they don't know what folks do when they're putting it together. They came out with clipboards and said the computer had gone down. I was in line. They said they needed to fill out the information manually because they need to keep track of who had the shots.

Anonymous 2021: Black life in Tucson, for me, has two elements: the secular and the religious/spiritual. The religious life is very stable in the sense that Blacks in Tucson group around commitments to either the Christian or Muslim congregations to which they belong. I see many Blacks experience their sense of (birthdays, funerals, weddings, graduations, etc.) mainly under the umbrella of their religious memberships. On the other hand, I do not see or experience a good range of the purely secular aspect of Black life in Tucson. One hears of the occasional jazz party at some club, or a concert at the Dunbar Pavilion. These are infrequent and not structured as recurring events.

I think the most important aspect of religious life for African Americans in Tucson today is the sense of commitment to the Church and fellowship. Many respond to the calls for help in sustaining the needs of the Church, and support (material and emotional) for members in trying times.

Yvonne Gathers, *Licensed social worker:* Remember, I told you I'm a social worker, so for many, many years when we were trying to help people in their environment and to move to a different level, experts kind of discounted the spiritual part of individuals' lives. I think in the last many years, I'd say in the last 30 years or so, we've realized that your spirituality is extremely important in gaining that sense of self, peace of mind, knowing who you are, giving you that self-confidence. Because I'm telling you, if I didn't have a spiritual self, I wouldn't even want to get out of bed in the morning. So, it just gives that sense of elevation. It gives you the strength to get up and tackle whatever you have to tackle every day. It gives you an "I can do it" kind of attitude. With me in my work, it helps me to realize that I can't fix anyone. It has to come from within individuals.

I worked for Child Protective Services for a while in Louisiana, which was my first time living in the South as an adult. I became the first Black social worker in this parish. So, when I look back over the years at the things that I have accomplished, you know academic kind of stuff, I attribute it all to my spiritual life, my spirituality. When I look at my family and how we came together … My son is going to be 50 in February, and we adopted him when he was two weeks old. Then I was blessed with a little girl two years later. So, I just feel like without my spirituality, and without other people's spirituality, I don't know how they get through life. Because there's so many things that's thrown at you, you don't know "Is it really me, or is it the color of my skin?" And so, when you have that kind of life "they see you before they know you" kind of feeling. I've been in that age group where you break down some barriers. It hasn't been easy. I'm not saying that. It's nowhere near as easy as maybe a skill of engineering or this or that. I have to account it all to my spirituality.

Lorna Ingram, *insurance agent, a business partner, and the vice president of the Tucson Progressive and Civic Club (National Association of Colored Women's Clubs):* The most important aspect is to be believers and to have faith. I'm seeing that more and more and more, that faith will get us through this. It brought us to; it will get us through this. I talk to a lot of my sister friends who are just holding on and [others] giving us hope. I like talking to the [last ones] because they give me hope, they inspire me; they uplift me, and that's important. They share the [gospel) Word, and the older they are, the more wisdom and experience you get from these people. It's amazing how they can just calm you down, you know? You smile when you see who's calling you, because they're going to be positive on purpose, and they're not going to bring a whole lot of negativity to your life. They're going to recognize and feed you the Word, and I do have two good friends that feed me the Word. Every single day, they sent me something and I was like "Wow! I needed that, right then and there." There are a lot of them; there are a lot of prayer warriors, which we need. They are great! I just admire these women, and I want to be like them!

John Greenwood, *Site supervisor at a behavioral health residential program:* I am a spiritual person. I am not a religious person. I just find religion to be corrupted, I believe in Our Creator. The Father, the Mother, the Universe. The Unknown. I don't have those answers. I think there's an obligation for us to try to make things better and be a positive contributor. So, I don't really dig church that much.

I've been involved in churches before. I had a good experience once recently in church for a couple years. Was just what I needed. I was getting a divorce and I got involved in this church. It was a United Methodist Church. All white people, like retired conservative folks way up in Catalina, and I was welcomed in with warm embrace—and my kids.

One thing I learned though is just that you have to kind of decide for yourself what you're going to do. It's more about what you do and how you live your life than what building you go to. I don't have an answer for that. I am more of a universal spiritualist, so I kind of look for good people to worship with. I try to make sure I stayed in good communication with the Creator daily. And I don't mind sharing that with other people in a group salutation or prayer, whatever.

Interviews about Life in Tucson 1990s and Before

What was the most important aspect of religious life for African Americans in Tucson?

Blanche Lucille Lewis: There were Sunday School picnics. The [Baptist Young Peoples Union] on Sunday evenings for the young teenagers. All the churches went together for sunrise service on Easter Sunday.

Marguerite Euell Sanchez, *Retired Tucson Unified School District librarian, former Dunbar school teacher:* Most people went to church. There were many programs, teas, lemonade parties, Heaven and Hell socials, signing conventions, etc. Everyone attended all the events at all the churches. It was a cross-denominational affair. Singers from Fisk University would come yearly

Catherine White Mize, *Long-time Tucson resident:* There were two churches—and everyone knew everyone by name and sight—everyone usually attended the same affairs.

Felix Goodwin, *retired Army lieutenant colonel, assistant to three University of Arizona presidents:* Everyone went to church (at Fort Huachuca). Deveaux was chaplain in the 40's.

Anonymous 1993: I belonged to the Catholic church and I served my religion. It was an obligation to belong to something. I went to Blessed Martin. They don't have it anymore. It was on Penn's place, but I don't think they call it Penn's place anymore. We weren't segregated. We could go to any church.

Dr. Laura Nobles Banks-Reed, *Educator, business owner, civic leader, and member of Alpha Kappa Alpha Sorority, Inc. and Tucson (AZ) Chapter of The Links, Incorporated:* Our lives pretty much revolved around our church and our activities.

African American Catholics in Tucson

From an Interview with Mona Mouton Blackburn by Tani Sanchez

When Blacks first came to Tucson, you could attend any Catholic church, but they [her parents and other African Americans] asked for their own. In the early '40s, a group asked the Bishop for Blessed Martin.

Father Vogel came as a request from Mother Mary Ellen Henley, who used to work with him in Los Angeles. He had been at another Black congregation. It was unusual in this area to have an African American church. Our congregation had maybe 25 families. It was a cohesive body of people, the whole group of us felt like family, Roberta Copeland, the Cole family, the Ross family, Barney Webb, and the Baptistes. We had all the weddings there and all the things churches do. In those days, the services were in Latin. I never felt separated because of race.

Editor's note: The Mouton family moved to Arizona in 1937. Mona's parents, Alcide and Laurice, were on their honeymoon in Tucson. When he was offered a job in the city, Alcide accepted and the couple relocated.

Holy Family Catholic Church was located directly adjacent to the segregated Dunbar School and within the formerly Black district. Several Black Catholics attended services there although its congregation was mostly Mexican American.

Recipes: Bread, Breaking It Together

William "Bill" Ponder, Board president of The Dunbar Coalition, Inc., Barbara Lewis, Dunbar Coalition vice president, and Desiree Gonzales, former Dunbar Coalition program manager..

Bread is beloved in many African American Tucson homes as it is in many others. Here are a few notes just for historical context. An agricultural, non-nomadic population with the ability to trade and store food goods has been considered a marker in the human transition from simple to more complex civilizations. The theory is that humans could develop more complex pursuits beyond basic survival. Arts and writing skills are examples. Although the rock arts of Australia and other older cultures show that nomadic humans had already abstracted complex symbolic ideas in rock and other arts, the move to an agricultural society is considered a bellwether stage in the flow of human development. The shock more recently has been that bread may have been part of human life for millennia even during hunter–gatherer periods. Prehistoric breadcrumbs suggest that Middle Eastern people made bread as early as 14,000 years ago, possibly as special treats.

Other popular breads made with corn have American Indian origins, but enslaved and free African Americans in the South added their own touches to cornbreads to suit their own palates, so not surprisingly there are a few cornbread recipes in this section. Dr. Jerome Dotson notes, "One of the reasons you see many corn-based breads among African Americans is also due to slavery. Some culinary historians argue that the predecessor to cornbread was a combination of water and ground corn that Black slaves learned from indigenous Americans in the Southeast."

Most recipes in this section are from past contributors, although one Cracklin' cornbread recipe is added to this second edition. Some contributors explained they were cutting back on making breads for health reasons or that the recipes they liked were either too complicated, or as in the case of one African man, because he preferred to purchase rather than make it at home. MyPlate, a U.S. Department of Agriculture website, explains that the issue involves refined versus whole grains. "Whole grains contain the entire grain kernel—the bran, germ, and endosperm. Examples of whole grains include whole-wheat flour, bulgur (cracked wheat), oatmeal, whole-grain cornmeal, and brown rice. Refined grains have been milled, a process that removes the bran and germ. This is done to give grains a finer texture and improve their shelf life, but it also removes dietary fiber, iron, and many B vitamins. Some examples of refined grain products are white flour, corn grits, white bread, and white rice."

CRACKLIN' CORNBREAD
Barbara Lewis

Cracklings are made from the crisp brown skin of ham rind or pork fat. However, my mother also made them from the skin of a chicken. Cut the rind or skin into small pieces and fry them in a skillet as you would bacon, until all the fat is removed and the pieces are brown and crisp. (This can also be done in the oven.)

Ingredients:

2 cups cornmeal

½ teaspoon salt

½ teaspoon baking soda

1 cup diced cracklings

1 cup buttermilk

Preheat oven to 425°F. Sift the dry ingredients together and rub/mix the cracklings in with your hands. Stir in the buttermilk. The batter will be a little stiff. You can either shape into oblong loafs and put on a greased baking sheet or use a 9″ × 9″ greased baking pan. Bake for 30 minutes or until lightly golden brown and firm to the touch. Serve hot.

PEPSI'S CORNBREAD
Pecolia L. Hayes

Ingredients:

1 cup flour

1 cup cornmeal

6 teaspoons baking powder

4 teaspoons sugar

½ teaspoon salt

2 eggs

1 cup milk

½ cup vegetable oil or bacon drippings

Mix dry ingredients in a large bowl. Add eggs, milk, and oil. Bake in 400°F oven for 25 minutes. Serves 6.

SPANISH CORNBREAD
Catherine White Mize

Ingredients:

1 cup flour	4 tablespoons fat, melted
1 cup cornmeal	1 egg
4 teaspoons baking powder	½ pound American cheese, grated
½ teaspoon salt	1 can whole-grain corn, 15 oz
1 cup milk	1 small green chili, diced

Mix all ingredients together. Pour batter into baking pan. Bake in 350°F oven for about 25 minutes.

Editor's note: if you use almond flour or a blend, sift to make sure it is not too heavy. Add corn extract to flavor. You can order corn extract online.

BUTTERMILK ROLLS
Elgie Batteau

Ingredients:

1 quart flour (4 cups)	1 yeast cake (0.6 ounces) or 1 packet of dry yeast
1 tablespoon salt, or less to taste	(see note)
½ teaspoon baking soda	2 cups buttermilk
½ teaspoon baking powder	1 egg
2 tablespoons sugar	Butter or oleo (margarine), melted, for brushing
3 tablespoons shortening	

Sift together all dry ingredients except sugar. Cream sugar and shortening. Dissolve yeast in buttermilk. Add egg to buttermilk and yeast. Mix well. Mix same as for biscuits. [Make a well in the dry ingredients, pour buttermilk mixture into the well, and mix with a fork until no dry spots remain and batter is well mixed.] Keep dough as soft as can be handled. Roll about ⅓-inch to ½-inch thick. Cut out with a biscuit cutter. Make an impression across each biscuit with the back of a knife; butter half of each biscuit, and fold them over to make Parker House rolls. Place rolls close together in an oiled pan. Brush tops of rolls with butter or oleo. Let rise 2 hours or more. Bake at 400°F until brown.

Editor's note: Oleo is an older term for margarine and almost never used today. Yeast cakes are also not common or as well known. In older times, fresh yeast was sold in the refrigerated section of some markets. Dry yeast has a longer shelf life. Yeast cakes are generally sold in either 2-ounce cakes or smaller 0.6-ounce cakes (one-third of the original 2-ounce size). If you are using a 2-ounce yeast cake, cut it in thirds and use one-third for this recipe. If you are using dry yeast, one packet of dry yeast equals one 0.6-ounce cake.

BUTTER ROLLS
Constance Smith

Ingredients:
2 packages dry yeast
1 cup lukewarm water
1 cup butter
½ cup sugar
1 teaspoon salt
1 teaspoon lemon flavoring
3 eggs
1 cup milk, scalded and cooled
about 7 cups flour, divided

Dissolve yeast in water. Cream butter, sugar, salt, and flavoring until light and fluffy. Add eggs one at a time, mixing well after each egg. Stir yeast mixture into milk. Beat milk with ½ cup of the flour until smooth. Blend in butter mixture. Add remaining flour gradually. Cover with damp cloth. Let rise somewhere warm (not hot) until double in bulk. Punch down. Turn dough out on floured board. Knead, roll out or shape as desired. Let rise on baking sheet until double in size. Bake about 15 minutes in 375°F oven.

Constance Smith was a teacher at John Spring Junior High and taught for 30 years. John Spring was the name given to the all-Black Paul Laurence Dunbar School after integration. She was active with many organizations including the NAACP, Alpha Kappa Alpha Sorority, Inc., and Prince Chapel African Methodist Episcopal Church.

Editor's note: Scalding mean heating the milk just short of the boiling point.

POTATO ROLLS
Enid Moore-Cranshaw

3 cakes yeast
10-1/2 cups sifted flour
4-1/2 tablespoons lard
1 cup sugar

4-1/2 teaspoons salt
3 eggs
3 cups milk
1-1/2 cup potato water

Heat milk and lard until lard is melted. Add potato water to the milk mixture. Cool mixture until lukewarm. Add eggs and yeast to mixture. Add mixture into sifted flour, sugar and salt. Knead on floured board until smooth. Place dough in a large greased deep pan or the bottom part of a roaster and brush with melted lard.

Cover with wax paper and let rise in a warm place until double in bulk. Punch down dough and let it rise again.

Form dough into small balls. Place three balls in each section of a muffin pans. Brush with melted lard; let dough rise again.   Bake in oven (375 degrees) from 20 to 25 minutes or until done.

Editor's note: Enid Moore-Cranshaw was the 2017-2018 District Director of Toastmasters International, District 3 and she served as the 2016 – 2018 Board President of Child Parent Services (Headstart). She is employed as a Financial Professional and owner of Divinity Salon.

FRIED BREAD (AMERICAN)
Hearon Hayes
Yield: 3 dozen

Ingredients:

1 cup milk	1 cup lukewarm water
5 tablespoons sugar	6 cups flour, divided
1 teaspoon salt	6 tablespoons melted shortening
1 package dry yeast	

Scald milk, add sugar and salt, and cool to lukewarm. While milk cools, dissolve yeast in lukewarm water. Add yeast mixture to cooled milk and add 3 cups of the flour. Beat until smooth, then add melted shortening and remaining flour. Mix well. Roll out on floured board to ¼″ thick. Cut into 3″ squares. Brown dough on both sides in hot oil.

Editor's note: Do NOT use a sugar substitute for yeast bread recipes or use at your own risk. The amount of sugar is generally minimal, and sugar is required for the bread to rise. The yeast will consume the sugars, reducing the impact.

FRIED BREAD (MEXICAN)
Hearon Hayes
Yield: 20 servings

Ingredients:

1¾ cups sifted all-purpose flour	2 tablespoons shortening
2 teaspoon baking powder	⅔ cup cold water
1 teaspoon salt	

Sift flour, baking powder, and salt into a mixing bowl. Cut in shortening coarsely. Add cold water gradually. Mix just enough to hold together. Turn out on lightly floured board and knead gently until smooth. Cover and let dough rest for 5 minutes. Roll out into a 12x5-inch rectangle. Dough should be very thin. Cut into 3″ squares. Drop a few squares at a time into deep hot oil. Turn squares over 3 or 4 times to make them puff evenly. Fry 2–3 minutes on each side or until golden brown. Serve hot as bread with honey.

Editor's note: Many contemporary recipes call for non-aluminum baking powder, eliminating any metallic taste. This powder causes the breads to rise immediately rather than waiting for moisture and heat. There really is a difference between fried breads. In my teens, during a summer Bible school session in Dallas, I met a white woman from Grand Rapids, Michigan, who seemed shocked that I knew nothing about the sweeter American version that she associated with Black people. She proceeded to make some for me. Her recipe used baking powder instead of yeast but it was quite good. No one contributed a recipe for American Indian frybread, but in Tucson I purchase it fresh whenever it is available. It is often sold by the roadside by individual vendors and cooked on the spot. It is a staple at a very limited number of restaurants.

BANANA NUT AND RAISIN BREAD
Pecolia L. Hayes

Ingredients:

2 medium bananas
2 eggs
1 cup sugar
⅓ cup vegetable oil
1 teaspoon vanilla

2 cups flour
2 teaspoon baking powder
1 cup raisins
½ cup walnuts

Mash bananas. Add eggs, sugar, oil, and vanilla. Mix well. Add flour. Beat in and add baking powder, raisins, and nuts. Bake at 350°F in loaf pan for about 50 minutes. Let cool on rack for about 10 minutes, then remove from pan to finish cooling.

Business and Employment

Jamillia Joseph is the owner of Dessert Island Eatery. Her Caribbean restaurant operated for many years in Tucson, but she relocated and reopened the Eatery in Phoenix. Photos on this page are from Jamillia Joseph.

The COVID-19 pandemic brought changes for many Black businesses, particularly for those serving foods. The pandemic compelled Caribbean food restaurant owner Jamillia Joseph to cancel the addition of a food truck. Other diasporic establishments such as Ceedee Jamaican Kitchen and D's Island Grill stayed in business along with Alafia West African Cuisine Beninese Restaurant.

Yevette Sykes, owner of Yevette's Food Affair Catering Company, operated a meal delivery service while continuing to work at a Black restaurant. Another person who seemed to thrive was Tina Marie Wilken. Local news outlets reported she began baking "decadent desserts" from her home, and Nosh Tucson, a bakery and catering service, was born. Similarly, Robb Walker, owner of AZ Fit Kitchen, made gluten-free doughnuts in his business's kitchen on Thursdays, and prepared healthy, complete meals for pickup, delivery and grab and go. Quiche and whole-grain pancakes are on his menu, along with salads and entrees such as BBQ Salmon w/Chipotle Lime, Red Quinoa Pilaf and Roasted Veggies. Some relatively longtime Black barbecue joints still exist, including Two Boots BBQ Shop, Smokey Mo, and Ken's Hardwood Barbecue. During summer 2021, Ken's sponsored a fundraiser with the Black sorority Delta Sigma Theta. All the barbecue restaurants had hand sanitizers, while Two Boots featured a sign admonishing guests to wait at the entry when physical distancing is needed.

Black residents also started the online Tucson Black Pages to increase the profile of Black-owned and operated businesses on the internet, saying, "We also hope to promote the use of Black businesses in Southern Arizona as well as the rest of our nation." At last review, the Tucson Black Pages website was a holding page, "being upgraded to better serve the community." Connected to BLAXFRIDAY.com, the website offered 14 categories of Arizona Black businesses such as apparel shops, legal services, real estate agents, doctors, hair professionals, restaurants, and bars that are easily accessible. Phoenix establishments dominate the Arizona site, but Nosh Tucson is listed.

Divinity Beauty Bar, a hair and nail establishment, opened in 2011, but the pandemic left some scars on the establishment. Forced to shut down for a few months, Enid Moore-Cranshaw, the owner, has had to reconfigure everything, adding physical distancing to the booths and lobby. She also started temperature checks on clients, questionnaires for new customers, and massive sanitizing of chairs. Her stylists change capes between each customer. The business offers a full range of services, such as silk presses, extensions, weaves, and coloring. As business comes back, Enid is planning to hire more stylists and people to do braids and nails. A finance and accounting graduate from Regis University, Enid also diversifies her haircare products, incorporating some manufactured goods from other Black businesses. "I am staying positive and trying to attract the right people," she says.

African American businesses have operated in the Old Pueblo for more than 100 years. From the late 1800s through the early 1900s, the barber profession was "all Black," remembers one resident. Arthur Lewis, Frank Denkins, and George Braggs all had their own shops and employed others.

Enid Moore-Cranshaw, owner of Divinity Beauty Bar, has one of the nicest, most posh salons in Tucson and offers "premium" services and products for all ethnic groups.

Dr. Andrew J. Johnson, a Chiropodist (Foot Doctor), opened his Tucson office in the Steinfeld Building in 1920 and practiced for many years. He was born in 1882 and died in 1950. Marguerite Euell Sanchez Collection.

Shoeshine parlors and eating joints were other enterprises. "Colored cooks," too many to mention, routinely worked in hotels in town—a Mr. Kindall, for example, cooked at the Santa Rita Hotel for many years, and Pete Rochon cooked at the Old Pueblo Club (then on Stone Avenue between Jackson and La Cholla). Mr. Mannings was one of the first Black people working at the University of Arizona, cooking food for professors and students.

The Southern Pacific Railroad hired Black people in significant numbers. Luscious Lyons, James Nobles, and William Glover worked for the railroads as machinists. Others worked in their shops, "repairing the tracks" and "doing all kinds of jobs." The most visible ones were redcaps—baggage handlers and porters.

The lure of mining brought others such as Charley Embers in 1866. Some, like George Wells, worked as carpenters. Sam Nobles worked for the county in road maintenance. Wiley Hayward, the first Black mail carrier, delivered mail using a horse and a two-wheeled cart. Creed Taylor was the chief engineer at the Desert Sanitarium.

By the 1930s, a typical wage was 25 cents an hour—but it was livable. One old timer noted, "you got a loaf of bread for a nickel, you got six cans of sardines for a quarter and then you paid about $3 a month for house rent!"

Probably the first Black professional to move to Tucson was Dr. A. B. Thompson, a medical doctor in the early 1930s who was regarded as the best in the state. A "spectacular" delivery at the Storks Nest, a popular birthing ward, had folks talking for days and months afterward. The story goes that he took a baby coming out feet first and turned it around in the womb and brought it out head first. According to one resident, Arizona Medical Association then turned around and invited him to join their ranks. One person says Thompson built everything he had from scratch in his first years, including his own operating table. Other medical practitioners of the 1930s included Dr. A, Johnson, a respected chiropodist, and an "herb doctor."

The years before and after World War II saw the establishment of more Black-owned businesses, most located on Meyer Street. Tommy Scott Cleaners and Peggy Watson's Chat and Chew Café became popular establishments. Jimmy's Chicken Shack also sold food and liquor, while a Meyer's Street pool hall caused some to see the neighborhood as a rough district. The "hot comb," for straightening black hair, swept the country in those days, and beauty shops sprung up—Blanchette Beauty Shop, owned by Blanche Johnson, being the first licensed one. A 1933 survey credits African Americans with owning three auto repair service stations, a wash rack, three restaurants, several shoe shine parlors, and other small businesses.

Naturally, African Americans bought from many merchants. Not forgotten by older residents are the medicinal items purchased from the Mexican-owned Tito's Pharmacy and foods sold by Chinese merchants.

Although local African Americans regularly subscribed to national "Negro" papers such as the *Chicago Defender* and the *Pittsburgh Courier* to keep informed of race issues, the Tucson newspapers, the *Arizona Call* and the *Arizona Register,* also provided news. The *Arizona Negro*

31 YEARS IN TUCSON

JACK'S
ORIGINAL BARBEQUE

"*Puts the Confidence Back*

FEATURING: *in Good Eating*"

BAR-B-Q BEEF • PORK • RIBS
• HAM • LINKS • PEACH COBBLER
• SWEET POTATO PIE

"LET US CUSTOM COOK YOUR MEAT"

Jack L. Banks - Owner

790-2351
5250 EAST 22ND

OPEN DAILY 11 A.M. - 9:30 P.M.
SUNDAY 12:00 - 8:30 P.M.

Jack and Dr. Laura Banks owned the restaurant. Jack served as a cook in the Army during World War II and was originally from Kansas. Ad from Marguerite Euell Sanchez Collection.

Journal—a weekly newspaper—documented information about soldiers at Fort Huachuca, local social activities and racial incidents. Headquartered at 167 South Meyer Street, the paper sold for 5 cents per copy in 1942.

In the 1960s and 70s, Park Avenue on the south side offered a multitude of enterprises, including hair salons, barbershops, corner stores and food establishments. In Sugar Hill, Jacks Original Barbeque was a popular Tucson institution on East Grant Road. It later relocated to East 22nd street. That property has been sold and owned several times, but a Black owned barbeque establishment has now been on the spot for several years.

Interviews about Contemporary Black Business and Employment

Jamillia Joseph, *owner of Dessert Island Eatery*: Initially we were supposed to be getting a food truck and do more outdoor events and we've thus far canceled the idea for the time being due to COVID-19. We were three months into opening in Phoenix when the pandemic hit, so we were not doing much networking. Now that we are experiencing a new norm, I am hoping to find ways to network with other business owners to be able to create a different type of experience for the community. I've found that in the present moment the only way to find our community is by way of customers that find us. The only thing that has changed for us is that we went from being a small dine-in restaurant to a to-go restaurant with the option to dine outside if you are comfortable in doing so. Our menu has stayed the same but will likely be downsized in the near future to help the kitchen to run smoother.

Debi Chess: We haven't been able to have events, haven't been able to book events. That's (Covid 19) been profoundly impactful to our organization. But it's also allowed us this down time to reach out. Like the Urban League; they've expressed a desire to be in our space and right now they've set up an office at the Dunbar. So, this down time has allowed us to kind of bring them on and look at ways to strengthen that relationship and do co-programming and things like that.

There aren't a lot of Black organizations in Tucson, so that's kind of difficult. There aren't a huge amount of them and in many ways, the Dunbar is the healthiest of all Black organizations. So, we're kind of looked at as *the* Black organization in Tucson. That's an interesting dynamic. Part of our move forward is bringing on more Black organizations into our space and looking at how we can help them support their sustainability and grow healthily. It's certainly part of our mission.

Reaching out has been really difficult in some regards. I think there's still a lot of trust that needs to be built amongst organizations. The universe has given us an opportunity wrapped in a terrible package, but we have to look inside of it for the gift, and that gift has been the opportunity to build, and reset, and realign missions and realign priorities. If we didn't take that approach to it, if we took a hysterical approach to it, we would be in the same place trying to keep the Dunbar afloat. So, I look at it as a gift. The virus is a horrible, horrible gift, sort of like an adversity. I think that's our charge.

Editor's note: The Dunbar Project launched in 1995 when The Dunbar Coalition, Inc. purchased the long-vacant Dunbar School building from Tucson Unified School District. The goal of the project is to renovate the 51,000-square-foot building into a museum and cultural center. TUSD closed the school in 1978 because of a desegregation lawsuit filed against it by Black families. In 2002, the renovation project received its initial grant of $900,000 from the federal government. In May 2004, the project was awarded another $1.2 million from a successful Pima County bond election.

Tina L. Johnson, *currently an administrative assistant at the University of Arizona and serves as a website content manager.* I came to Tucson in 1994. My goal was to earn a graduate degree so that doors could open for me and I could do different things in life and I could earn some money. I was literally leaving Boston, Massachusetts. I came to Tucson with my two 10-year-old kids and three suitcases and started over. I knew I could focus on raising my two kids. My goal was to get a degree, get a good job, and see that they were raised happy and had opportunities. Life here was good. I eventually got a job and they were in school and I wanted that they would not be uprooted again from friends and family. And then they went to high school and I was in school at the same time. I was a full-time student and a part-time worker and I lived on that salary, and that was very challenging. I finally got a job, senior development director at the UA Foundation.

Actually, being a Black person in Tucson, it was very challenging. I could not immediately find a job after I did graduate. Doors were just not opening, and I was very discouraged about that. And the only reason I got a job was I attended a conference where Slivy Edmonds Cotton, Jacqueline Monk, and Edie Auslander talked about how they made it. They had mentoring; they were able to do things. They talked about networking. And I stood up and I said, "I'm looking for a job. Are you all available? How do you make this work?" I'm in this whole big old conference room, and I said I'm ready, I need this. If Slivy had not come back and found me a job over on campus, I don't know where I would be today. It was held over at the U of A and the Student Union. It was for the Commission on the Status of Women. Speaking of which, I am a member of the Commission on the Status of Women now too. It was either be bold or be broke and not have my kids have a roof over their heads. They were talking about ways in which women should be empowering themselves, making decisions, trying to do things. And I had to put it to the test. Either you're talking or you're not. Are you really going to do something?

Algurie Wilson, *President Coalition for African American Health and Wellness.* I was really excited about it because now there is a focus on supporting Black businesses. I think that is so key, because when I first got here, we tried to get involved and my husband [Bernard] got involved. They had the Black Chamber of Commerce, so I was all excited. I think it is so key for us to start supporting and helping each other.

What early Black businesses and professionals did you patronize?

Dr. Laura Nobles Banks-Reed: As a child I remember Black beauty and barber shops. I can also remember very small cafes (sometimes no more than holes in the wall.) Mr. White and Barbara's Bar-B-Q Pit was very popular. We used to jitterbug on a slab in the rear of the store.

Blanche Lucille Lewis: Barber shops, beauty shops, cafes, shoe-shining parlors. The most popular was the beauty shop.

Constance Smith: Corner grocery store [on the south side], beauticians, barbers, cafes, Elks club.

Marguerite Euell Sanchez: Beauty parlors—most were in homes before Blanche Johnson. On Meyer Street, Bernice Johnson and Tossie Lee Moore were in business. The Elks, Jimmy's Chicken Shack, the Chat & Chew and various others were on Meyer Street. Tito Flores' pharmacy and cafe was popular; it was owned by a Mexican.

Anonymous 1993: The American Legion was run by Blacks. They entertained; they had a band with Claytie Lokey. She was a piano player. She was very popular.

A Black Businesswoman Remembers

Portions of an Interview with Blanche Johnson by Tani Sanchez

I came here in 1936 from Little Rock, Arkansas. My sister Julia was already here and she wanted me to come out because she saw the possibilities. They didn't have any beauty business here. They had two women doing the beauty work in their houses—one was Bessie Kilmer—but there wasn't any beauty shop here. They only had one beauty school and they wouldn't accept more than two Blacks at a time. I went to apply and they told me they already had their quota. And they told me I could wait a year or two and try to get in. Instead of doing that, I went on to Ruth's Beauty School in Los Angeles, a Black school. Nine months later, I took my state board. I opened my shop and was the first to have a license and take the state board.

I was in business for almost 33 years. I established my shop at 305 West 6th Street: Blanchette Beauty Salon. My husband gave me my first $100. His uncle helped me, and my sisters. My sisters gave me the privilege of using the rental property. Julia owned property, an eight-room house with a small rental in back. My brother was visiting from Arkansas and he helped me set it up. Thelma Hardin, she was a member of the state board, she gave me the privilege of using her old furniture until I got my new furniture. She was white, and opened a shop near the university.

Later, I was one of the first instructors at Walker's Beauty School. It was for Black people, and soldiers went too. They had a nice group of students. We taught how to do white hair, Black hair, everybody. Maureen Craft was one of the first to graduate. Glamor Girls North Fourth and Fifth streets was an integrated school, too.

When I first came here, it wasn't too much excitement or entertainment. Julia was in one of the plays called *The Women* and it was at the Temple of Music and Art. Julia Williams was in a lot of plays at the university. She encouraged others to come to the university. One thing about the university, you didn't have too many [Black people] people out there. The Eureka Club is one of the oldest clubs here as far as Blacks go. The Gay Modern Matrons, they used to have plays and parties. Then the Jolliett's gave social dances. If you belonged to the clubs, they gave formals, and it was all dress up. There was the Elks, the Dugout, and the American Legion. They were sponsoring out-of-town orchestras to come down here. They played in the Black clubs on Meyer Street. Duke Ellington played at Tucson High. They had to guarantee them a certain amount of money, but they did pretty good. And over to the church I remember them having nice plays, several church plays. One of the plays was called *The Garden of Eden*. They didn't have but three churches then: Mount Calvary, Prince Chapel, and Phillips C.M.E. On Congress there was Chinese food, Perkins Cafe, and Richy Lou's. Anybody could go there. On Stone Avenue, the Fox Theater; and another on East Congress where everybody could usually go. It might have been the Lyric. We had to be segregated. They had the American Legion and the Elks Club and the Dugout and Jimmy's Chicken Shack. We had to go to the places on Meyer Street. It was partly segregation.

Hosea and Blanche Johnson, Marguerite Sanchez collection

From the Old Pueblo Club to the Ghost Ranch Lodge

Portions of an Interview with Hosea Johnson by Tani Sanchez

In the 1940s, I worked at the Old Pueblo Club on Stone Avenue and Jackson Streets. It was a club that was owned and operated by the businessmen of the city. I had other cooks working under me, some Blacks and one white. I was the menu man. Steaks, filet mignon, New York cuts, braised short ribs. In the 1950s, I worked at the Ghost Ranch Lodge. Mulligatawny soup, I made it up myself out of my head. I had a little nutmeg in that soup.

Editor's note: Mulligatawny soup came into being as a result of colonialism in India as cuisines and outside tastes were accommodated. Eventually, mulligatawny soup with "roots in Indian cuisine" would be perceived as British. Another origin explanation is that the soup came into being during India's colonization in the mid-1800s, when "British soldiers stubbornly refused to alter their way of dinning, requiring a soup at the start of the meal." There are many modern versions of the dish across the globe and Hosea's addition of nutmeg is one example. In terms of the Old Pueblo Club, the Arizona Historical Society has posh images of the club in the 1960s. They feature a winding staircase, chandeliers, and table seating next to top floor windows with views of the city. All the patrons pictured are white and appear to be upper class. Similarly, the Ghost Ranch Lodge at one time was a tourist friendly site. Designed by a renowned local architect, and "owned by Arthur Pack, co-founder of the Arizona-Sonora Desert Museum." This interview makes me think of the "invisible" Blacks who worked behind the scenes.

Recipes: Main Dishes, Poultry and Seafood, Vegetarian

VEGAN CURRY CHICK'N & POTATOES
Jamillia Joseph
A vegan twist on Caribbean Curry Chicken & Potatoes

Yield: 2–4 servings

Jamillia Joseph, owner of a Caribbean restaurant, says, "I love jollof and I try to use the technique and the ingredients of the base to create vegan dishes for the family. However, every island cooks different. For example, I know in Trinidad some tend to use tomatoes or ketchup in some of their curry dishes; that's not something that we do. I try to utilize ideas from different islands based on what we like. An example is our blended green seasoning. I do believe all islands have their own version. We also prepare our own pepper sauce, jerk BBQ sauce, and jerk dry rub. Jerk is more of a Jamaican thing, and we've managed to have created some recipes using our own techniques that allows us to present our version of jerk dishes. I was born in Jamaica but am more comfortable saying that I am Caribbean because I was not raised there and my knowledge of it is very little."

Prep 15 minutes. Cook 20 minutes. Ready in 35 minutes.

Ingredients:

4 to 6 king oyster mushrooms, shredded (about 2½ cups)

2½ cups cubed potatoes

1 tablespoon grapeseed oil

2 teaspoons minced garlic

1 teaspoon minced ginger

¼ cup diced onion

2 teaspoons diced green pepper

1 tablespoon + ½ teaspoon curry powder

¼ teaspoon cumin

2½ cups water

½ cup coconut milk

1 tablespoon of fresh cilantro

2¼ teaspoons sea salt

2 sprigs of fresh thyme

1 bay leaf (optional)

¼ teaspoon dried oregano

¼ teaspoon dried parsley

¼ teaspoon poultry blend

pinch of ground rosemary (optional)

3 pimento seeds (optional)

Scotch bonnet or habanero pepper to taste (optional)

Shred king oyster mushrooms using a fork. Peel and cut potatoes and put them in a bowl of water to soak. Heat grapeseed oil in a pot on medium heat. Once oil is heated, add the garlic, ginger, onions, and green peppers and let cook until onions begin to turn translucent, about 4 minutes.

Add curry powder and cumin for about 45 seconds while stirring, then add water and coconut milk. If curry is left in the oil for too long it will burn. Add remaining ingredients and cook on medium-high until the potatoes are cooked, about 10–12 mins.

JAMAICAN ACKEE AND SALTFISH
Geta LeSeur-Brown, professor emerita

Dr. Geta LeSeur-Brown is a retired professor of English and Africana Studies from the University of Missouri and the University of Arizona. She is a "pure Jamaican" who came to Tucson in the early 1970s after getting her degrees from Columbia and Indiana universities and receiving major academic awards such as a Fulbright to Spain. Her second book, Not All Okies are White: The Lives of Black Cotton Pickers in Arizona, focuses on the small Black town of Randolph. It was selected as is the "Southwest Best Book" in 2020. Her husband, Ed Brown, was a star athlete at the University of Arizona and the first Black head football coach in Southern Arizona. He left a strong impact after 29 years at Cholla High School where the stadium is named for him. He is also in the Pima County Sports Hall of Fame and the UA Sports Hall of Fame.

Ingredients:

1-2 pounds salted codfish (also known as Bacalao)

4-6 slices bacon, chopped

¼ cup coconut or other cooking oil

1 large onion, sliced

1 teaspoon garlic, minced

2 onions or scallion stalks, chopped

2 tomatoes, sliced

1 teaspoon black pepper or to taste

1-2 Scotch bonnet peppers, or other peppers such as jalapeno. Scotch Bonnet is the most common and hottest. Use sparingly the first time.

2 (18- ounce) cans ackee, drained

Soak saltfish in warm water overnight to get the salt out, but you must leave some of the salty taste in it. Drain and keep pouring out the water. Use just enough water to cover. If the saltfish has bones, then you can debone. Slowly boil on medium fire a few minutes. Don't overcook. Flake the fish afterwards. Set aside.

Fry the bacon in a large skillet and then set aside, leaving drippings in the skillet. Add onions to skillet drippings and sauté. Fold in tomatoes and sauté for a few minutes. Add saltfish and sauté for a few minutes. Top with ackee and also cook a few minutes. Let cool. Serve with your choice of white rice, green bananas, plantains, squash, or bread. adjust the seasoning to taste. Remove your ackee and saltfish from the heat and let it cool. You may prepare this a day in advance. Add ready-made hot sauce, if desired. Use the brand you prefer.

Dr. LeSeur-Brown says "Saltfish, the preferred name by West Indians, is also known as cod fish. It can be purchased deboned or boned, but a real islander would not dare do {debone} that!" She warns, "Fixing this dish takes constant watching every step."

Editor's note: Ackee is a fruit and this dish is often considered a breakfast meal although it can be eaten at any time. There are some health warnings against *fresh* ackee which is not sold in the states. However, the canned ackee in this recipe meets FDA standards and is available from Amazon.com and other places.

TWO GUMBOS: ONE CREOLE, ONE CAJUN
Petra Robertson

Petra says creole gumbo has a tomato base and is more of a soup, while Cajun gumbo has a roux base and is more of a stew. Prep time 2 hours. You will need a large soup or tamale pot.

Creole Gumbo Ingredients:
3 to 4 pounds of shrimp (whatever size you like raw shell on)
5 cups of low-sodium chicken broth
2 14.5-ounce cans petite diced tomatoes (with juice)
2 bottles clam juice (optional)
¼ cup creole seasoning (see ingredient note)
cayenne pepper to taste (optional)
6 stalks of celery, diced
1 sweet onion, diced
1 bell pepper, diced
5 cloves of garlic, minced
2 tablespoons chopped parsley
½ stick of butter
1 tablespoon extra-virgin olive oil
2½ to 4 pounds of chicken wings, sectioned, *or* 3 to 6 chicken breasts, cooked and cubed
1 to 2 packages smoked sausage, sliced and cooked

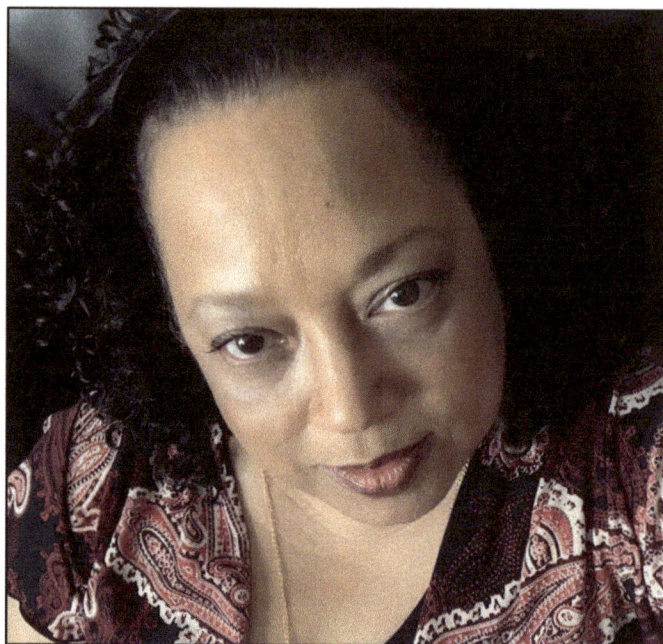

3 to 4 pounds of snow crab legs, *or* canned crab, if you prefer
canned or fresh oysters and/or clams (optional; if used, these should be added with the raw shrimp)
1 tablespoon gumbo file powder, or to preference (a thickening agent; add near the end of cooking)
chopped green onion for garnish (optional)
cooked rice

Peel and devein the shrimp; keep the shells and set the shrimp aside in the fridge for later. Rinse shells and put them and enough water to cover them in a pot to boil. When the shells turn pink, lower to simmer for 5 minutes. Strain the shell broth into the gumbo pot and toss the shells in garbage. This intensifies the shrimp flavor in the gumbo.

Add all liquids, seasonings and canned items to the gumbo pot, bring to a boil, then lower to simmer.

Chop all veggies or blend in blender—celery, onion, bell pepper, garlic, parsley. If blending, add a little water to make the blending easier. In a skillet, heat olive oil and sauté veggies just until they become soft or, if blended, just until you can smell the aroma of the veggies. Add to the gumbo pot. At this point you can taste the broth to adjust your cayenne levels. Adjust as needed. If you are really looking for some flavor, you can kick things up by adding an additional ¼ cup of creole seasoning to make it a full ½ cup.

In a skillet, heat butter and olive oil and brown chicken. Put browned chicken in gumbo pot. In the same skillet, place 2 ladles of gumbo broth to deglaze the pan, stirring it to get all the good stuff off the bottom. Strain this into the gumbo pot. Bring the gumbo pot to a boil and then lower it to a simmer. In a skillet,

brown the sliced sausage; place cooked sausage on paper towels to drain oil. Put the prepared sausage and the file in the gumbo pot. Cook for 20 minutes stirring occasionally.

Clean crab legs, if using. Add shrimp, crab legs and any canned seafood, and cook until shrimp are done. Once finished, serve over rice with green onion garnish and a side of toasted French bread. So delicious!

Creole seasoning can be found in the seasoning aisle at your local grocery store.

Cajun Gumbo: Use the same basic ingredients, but omit the tomatoes; some people add okra. I like to use Louisiana Cajun gumbo base. I can usually find it in the store but sometimes I get it from Amazon.com.

Petra says of her cooking these days, "I do cook lower fat. For instance, I don't use flours for gravies or anything like that. I tend to use a cornstarch slurry because that's not as fattening. I have to admit, I'm sorry, but I have to have my fried chicken. But really, I do all kinds of food. I do Japanese food, I do Korean food, Chinese food, Filipino food. So, my cooking is quite diverse, and I try not to be heavy with gravies and things like that."

Editor's note: The Harvard School of Public Health says, "Fish and other seafood are the major sources of healthful long-chain omega-3 fats and are also rich in other nutrients such as vitamin D and selenium, high in protein, and low in saturated fat. There is strong evidence that eating fish or taking fish oil is good for the heart and blood vessels." They recommend that people eat fish twice a week. The California Office of Environmental Health Hazard concurs with the benefits but offers this caveat, "While eating fish has nutritional benefits, it also has potential risks. Fish can take in harmful chemicals from the water and the food they eat. Chemicals like mercury and PCBs can build up in their bodies over time."

As an aside, my grandmother, Mary Wright Euell, born in Louisiana, made a special New Year's Eve seafood gumbo that she served at an elegant party to mark the beginning of the year. It was such an exquisite culinary treat! While living in New Orleans as an adult for a few years, I came to understand Creole referred to the very urban culture of Black/mixed-race people. Cajun was considered white and more rural.

DIRTY ROOT GUMBO
Anton Russell

Photo by Anton

Prepare this dish as a ritual, with the intention to eat it in community celebration. A ritual like the acknowledgment of the fullness of your blessings on a full moon or the calling in of intention-setting on a new moon; a celebration simply being that you have people in your life to share love and abundance. Turn on the music, get out the cutting board (and wine if that's yo thang) and move your body while chanting, moanin' and sangin'!

Ingredients:

1 quart of vegetable stock (beef or chicken stock or bone broth may be substituted)

Roux (see instructions)

1 pound okra, sliced

1 large *or* 2 medium onions (one red and one sweet), diced

1 bunch green onions, sliced

1 large (28 ounce) can crushed tomatoes, *or* 2 to 3 tomatoes, diced

2 sprigs parsley, chopped

1 package soy chorizo (Trader Joe's is on point)

1 bay leaf

pinch of file (gumbo file)

Roux: Roux is one part to one, so 2 tablespoons of flour to 2 tablespoons plant butter, and so on for larger batches (regular butter is non-vegan). There is room to get fancy with seasonings here but no pressure; the roux is here to give the gumbo that base. Heat butter very low so that it does not burn the butter and then add flour. This takes a while to get it amber brown, so music and dancing! Just keep stirring.

That dirty part? We need to bring in the harvest from your garden. Carrots, kale, radishes? Wash them lightly from handling, slice up the roots and slide them, soil and all, into the pot! Why? Take some time to observe the link between our blood and the soil that nourishes the roots of plants. Take some time to observe how Africans were trafficked to the Americas as master agriculturalists (still unpaid). Also, get ready to thrill your inner child that loved the taste of dirt!

1. Set your pot or Crock-Pot to low. Gumbo will do its thang while you sleep, and you have to let all of this sit at least a day before sharing (as is custom). Add the stock to the pot. Prepare the roux and add that while you call in your chosen ritual or point of reflection. If you are using shrimp, add it now.

2. Get out your cutting board and turn up! Call in your intention. Appreciate the colors of the harvest from Earth, and look to have a diverse setting—red, gold, purple, green … Prepare as instructed, and if you add things just make them small mouth bite size.

Some of these veggies are real nice with a singe on 'em first. If you do this, start bigger and come down to diced. This is one place you make it your own, or different each time. For example: Add okra, onions, celery this time; next time leave out the celery and add green onions.

3. Using the same skillet as the roux, make the soy chorizo (or choice of meat) and slide it into the pot.

4. Seasoning! Again, this is all about you! We will feel your vibration from your intention-setting best if I do not guide your hand in that spice rack. Do not be afraid to explore, but I advise all newcomers to invest in a good seasoning mix to get acquainted with the creole palette. Tony Chachere's or Cajun's Choice are both available at Sprouts and they list their ingredients, so you can start there and make it your own.

Add water or stock as needed to ensure all things are completely submerged. Hug yourself and hold your hands while turning your smile inside. Tenderly love each part of the whole you that just did this thang! Share with those for whom appreciation is shared!

Anton Russell is the program director at The Drawing Studio, which is a non-profit arts organization. He writes and hosts rap performances and has served as the secretary for the NAACP. Anton says, "I am a writer, I've been since I was a child. It is a form of wellness. If I don't write I won't live, so it is a big part of who I am and what I do. Beyond that I work in our community. I have been a community activist since 1995 doing all kinds of things, primarily focusing on working with youth and working with those that have been impacted—Black folk in particular—who have been impacted by racists, by the targeted violence against our bodies, against our communities. I create spaces, and I facilitate spaces wherein, one, area folk can learn how those impacts are real and can be educated so that hopefully they can do something with that education and, two, in another space completely elevate those voices of those that have been harmed so that we can talk about the ways that we can seek to be compensated for our damages, and so in spaces that are brave and somewhat safe where we can articulate how we've been impacted."

Editor's note: Singe refers to a char, a surface burn.

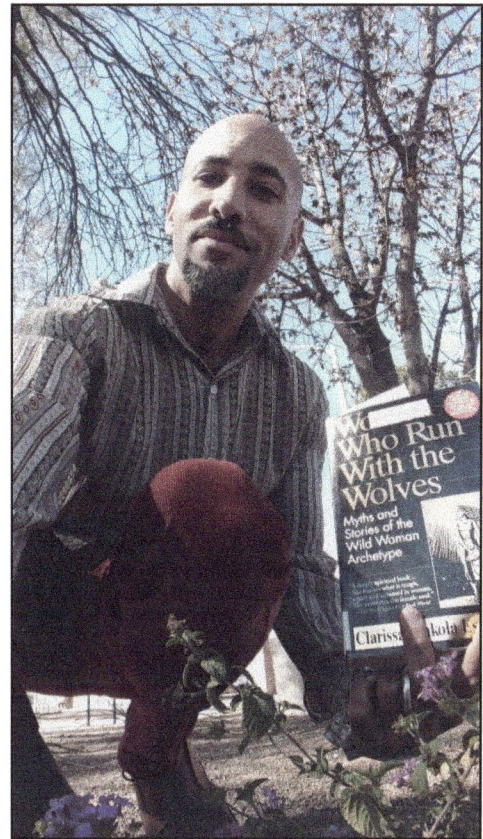

ALCIDE MOUTON'S FAMILY GUMBO
Mona Mouton Blackburn

Ingredients:

1 pound okra	2 sprigs parsley
4 tablespoons oil	4 bay leaves
2 tablespoons flour	2 quarts water
2 onions, chopped	1 tablespoon salt
1 bunch green onions, chopped	1 teaspoon cayenne pepper
1 cup of chopped celery	1 pound raw shrimp
4 cloves garlic, minced	3 or 4 cleaned crabs
1 (16-ounce) can tomatoes	1 pound beef sausage (optional)

Fry okra in 2 tablespoons oil for about 15 minutes. Season and fry only until brown. Add salt and pepper. In another pan, mix flour and remaining oil until it is as brown as coffee grinds. Do not let this burn; if it does, start over. Add onions, green onions, celery, and garlic. Cook 5 minutes, until vegetables are soft. Add fried okra. Stir in tomatoes, parsley, bay leaf, and water. Simmer 30 minutes. Add washed, deveined, and peeled shrimp and cleaned crabs. Simmer 30 minutes longer. If you prefer not to use okra, omit and use file seasoning instead.

SEAFOOD CAJUN GUMBO
Hearon Hayes

Ingredients:

1 chicken, 3 pounds or more, cut up	Salt and pepper to taste
Lard or oil for frying	Cayenne pepper to taste
1 cup flour	1 pint of oysters, *or* 1 pound of shrimp
1 large onion, chopped	1 14.5oz can okra
2 cloves garlic, minced	2 tablespoons minced parsley
2 quarts water	¼ teaspoon thyme
2 cups diced ham (the best flavor comes from old-fashioned salty ham)	

Brown chicken pieces in lard or oil. Season them well with salt and pepper; set aside.

Add flour to cooking fat; cook and stir to create a deep brown roux. Add onion and garlic, cooking them in the roux until tender. Add water, ham, and browned chicken. Simmer gently until ham and chicken are tender. Season well with salt, pepper, and cayenne. Add oysters or shrimp, okra, parsley, and thyme for last few minutes only. Don't cook mixture too much after adding the okra or it will become gummy. However, gumbo may be kept warm in the pot or a chafing dish. Serve with fluffy rice, French bread, and red wine.

CAJUN CATFISH
Beverely Elliott

Ingredients:

Fresh catfish

2 cups of yellow cornmeal

1 tablespoon Cajun seasoning

1½ cups corn oil

½ cup Butter Flavor Crisco

Salt and pepper to taste

Clean catfish. Salt and pepper to taste. Combine cornmeal and Cajun seasoning in a bowl. Dip and toss catfish pieces in cornmeal mixture to coat. Heat oil and Crisco in a skillet. Place coated catfish in hot oil. Cook or fry for 10 minutes, turning every 2–3 minutes.

Editor's note: Crisco is a solid all-vegetable shortening. It has a high melting point. All shortenings are thick, because they're solid at room temperature. This is in contrast to oils, which are liquid at room temperature. Shortening originally meant lard. Vegetable shortening was a 19th century invention. Oil or butter can sometimes be used as substitutes.

CHICKEN CROQUETTES
Brena Andrews

Brena Andrews is the instructional Designer with the College of Veterinary Medicine at the University of Arizona. She manages different tech-related projects through the center and also coaches track and field for high school students.

Ingredients:

1 cup diced cooked chicken breast

1½ cup Panko bread crumbs, divided

½ cup chopped mushroom

¼ cup minced sweet onion

¼ cup minced celery

¼ cup milk

1 egg

1 tablespoon minced garlic

Prepare chicken breast using desired method (baked, fried, etc.) and dice. Set aside ½ cup of bread crumbs for tossing. Combine the rest of the bread crumbs (1 cup), the chicken, and the remaining ingredients in a large mixing bowl and mix thoroughly until a doughy texture is accomplished. Use your hand to form balls or patties the size of your palm and place, separated, on a cookie sheet. Chill uncovered in the refrigerator for 15–20 minutes.

Working quickly, toss each chilled patty in the breadcrumbs that were set aside and replace on the cookie sheet. Cover and let chill in the refrigerator 6–8 hours or overnight.

SELMA EUELL OLIVER'S GARLIC ROASTED CHICKEN
Selma Euell Oliver

Garlic develops a mellow flavor when roasted. Herbed garlic butter, spread under the skin of the chicken, bastes the meat with flavor as it roasts.

Ingredients:

1 whole fryer chicken

20 garlic cloves – 10 peeled and pressed, 10 unpeeled

2 tablespoons butter or margarine
½ teaspoon grated lemon peel
¼ teaspoon dry thyme leaves

⅛ teaspoon dry rosemary leaves
2 thin slices lemon
Pinch of salt and pepper

Peel and press 10 garlic cloves. Combine butter, pressed garlic, lemon peel, thyme, and rosemary and mix to make garlic butter.

Starting at breast bone, carefully work fingers under skin of chicken, around breast and legs. Spread garlic butter under the skin. Place 10 unpeeled garlic cloves and the lemon slices into the body cavity. Season chicken lightly with salt and pepper. Place in a roaster and cover with foil. Bake at 375°F 1¼ to 1½ hours.

To serve: Remove garlic cloves from cavity. Peel and serve with chicken or blend with butter and use as a spread for thick slices of French bread.

For outdoor cooking, roast chicken in a covered grill over indirect medium heat between 1 and 2 hours, or on a rotisserie for 1 to 2 hours.

LEFTOVER WEDNESDAY CHICKEN
Edria Johnson

Ingredients:
4 chicken quarters (thighs and legs)
¼ stick butter
1 tablespoon olive oil
1 yellow onion, chopped
3 garlic cloves, minced, *or* 1 tablespoon of minced garlic from a jar
1 green bell pepper, chopped
1 red bell pepper, chopped
2 celery stalks, chopped (or more if you like a lot of celery)
2 tablespoons Italian seasoning
1 tablespoon dried basil
2 small bay leaves
1 box chicken stock (about 4 cups)
2 cans diced tomatoes, with their juices, plus any

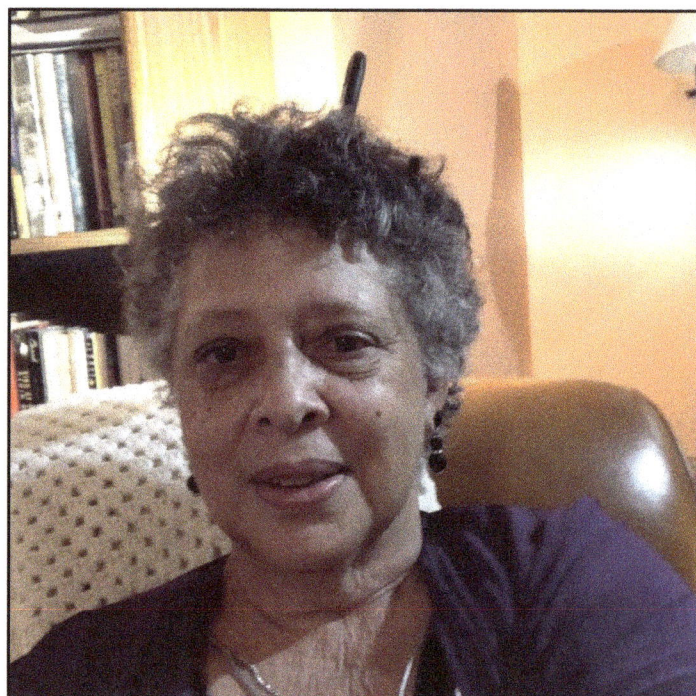

tomatoes you have in the refrigerator going soft (scoop out the seeds in the fresh tomatoes and dice them)
Pasta of your choice (I like the veggie pasta because it adds color to your plate, and it is delicious.)
salt and pepper to taste.

Clean the chicken pieces. Remove the skin and fat from the thighs and the fat from the legs. If the thighs and legs are still connected, cut them in half. This should result in 8 pieces of chicken. Rub salt and pepper on chicken parts and set aside.

Using your skillet, slowly melt olive oil and butter. Please melt slowly so the butter will not burn. Brown all chicken pieces uniformly; this should only take about 5 minutes. If your skillet is small, do this in batches. You do not want to crowd the chicken. Remove the browned chicken and place it in the Crock-Pot.

Sauté vegetables and garlic in skillet about 3 minutes; you do not want to overcook. Season with Italian seasoning and basil. Add vegetables to the Crock-Pot. Add bay leaves, stock, and tomatoes. The Crock-Pot should only be about half full. Set timer on low for about 6 hours.

Before I serve, I remove the bay leaves. I also cook pasta as indicated on the box. If you do not like pasta, rice, and potatoes actually taste incredibly good with this chicken sauce. I love removing a few cups of sauce and adding one cup of marsala to the sauce. I simmer until the alcohol burns off and then combine with the original sauce and chicken; it is heavenly. I serve with a spinach salad and hot Italian garlic bread.

Edria Johnson retired from American Airlines and is socially active. She says, "Chicken was a favorite in my family and inexpensive, so we had it quite often. I would take whatever vegetables were left in the refrigerator and combine it with whatever chicken I had left, add tomatoes and the trinity (onions, green bell peppers and celery) and we had a meal over rice. This was the Wednesday meal. My children are all grown now and have lives of their own, but I still love my "Leftover Wednesday Chicken." I made some changes over the years and it has evolved into a meal I serve with wine and pasta. This version uses a Crock-Pot and a skillet for browning. Please keep in mind the amounts are estimates. I have used this recipe many ways over the years and I do not measure these ingredients."

Editor's note: Dried vegetable pastas are great alternatives! The base for these pastas can be yellow peas, chickpeas, lentils, and so on. They are available in grocery stores or online. For me, there is no significant difference in taste for dried vegetable pastas. Fresh vegetable substitutes like zucchini do taste differently but work as well. I like those zucchini faux pastas (zoodles) that can be purchased in the refrigerated section or made at home by cutting fresh zucchini noodles with a vegetable peeler or special spiralizer. You can buy cutters in stores. Carrots and cucumbers are other choices to consider. Miracle Noodles are also a choice; these have no carbs or calories and the base is the konjac plant from Asia. Some people swear by these.

BARBECUED STUFFED CORNISH HENS
Constance Smith
Ingredients:
6 cleaned Cornish hens, *or* broiler chickens

For sauce:

1 cup salad oil	½ cup red wine
1 large onion, chopped	1 tablespoon Tabasco sauce
6 cloves garlic, diced	2 tablespoons salt
2 lemons, halved and sliced thinly	1 tablespoon brown sugar
1 bottle tomato ketchup	1 tablespoon oregano
1 cup water	1 teaspoon black pepper
1 cube bouillon	Dash of red pepper
1 cup white vinegar	

For stuffing:

½ pound butter	2 pounds fresh mushrooms

½ cup minced celery leaves   salt and pepper to taste
1 tablespoon paprika

Sauce: Place salad oil in a large, deep skillet. Add onion and garlic. Simmer for 20 minutes. Remove from heat and add sliced lemon. Return to burner and add ketchup, water, bouillon cube, vinegar, wine, and Tabasco sauce. Let mixture simmer slowly, adding salt, brown sugar, oregano, black pepper, and red pepper.

Season hens with salt and pepper, inside and out. Marinate well with the sauce.

Stuffing: Melt butter in skillet and allow to brown slightly. Add mushrooms, celery leaves, paprika, and salt and pepper to taste. Sauté for 15 minutes.

To cook: Stuff each hen and place close together on pit or spit. Cook over very low charcoal for 3 hours.

Editor's note: A pit refers to meat that is cooked below ground. A spit refers to meat that is skewered and roasted. Another trick I learned for recipes that use wine is to make sure you use a wine you like!

BLANCHE JOHNSON'S CHICKEN

Ingredients:
1 nice big fryer chicken (must be thawed)
Salt and pepper to taste
Seasoned salt
Flour
Margarine

Put salt and pepper inside and around chicken. Place chicken in a 350°F oven in a roaster (or any deep pan) for at least 1 hour. When brown, lift the chicken out and make gravy in the same pot by sprinkling flour to thicken drippings, adding margarine and let brown. Add more water if needed.

Editor's note: Mrs. Johnson fixed this for friends and relatives and they told her no one makes this chicken the way she does.

THE LAST BODY OF ROAD DOGG
Anton Russell
A vegan taco/fajita

Ingredients:
Tortillas   Peppers (optional)
Chickpeas, canned   Curry powder
Potatoes   Salt and pepper
Celery   Turmeric
Onions

There's a vegan dish that I put together and it's called The Last Body of Road Dogg. Essentially what you do is you get a tortilla, preferably 3 or 4 tortillas from La Estrella Bakery at South 12th Avenue, 12th and Irvington Road, so it's local. You take the tortilla, that's the base. Now what I do [for the filling is] is I take chickpeas, potatoes, celery, onions—both of them, like green onions as well as either a sweet white or red onion depending on what your own personal flavor is—and then you can add peppers if you would like to. If some people don't like spice, we can leave the pepper part out. But there is an assortment of spices that will add to it beyond that, which are curry, salt, and pepper, and I add some turmeric, because I like the color that leaves it nice and yellow. Put these ingredients, not the tortillas, in a sauce pan and bring to a boil with the liquid from the chickpea can, then simmer on low for about 15 minutes.

Editor's note: Tortillas are a popular flat Mexican bread. The American Institute for Cancer Research says, "Beyond calories, nutritional value depends on whether the tortillas are made with whole grains and healthy fats. Instead of flour tortillas made from enriched flour (a refined grain), look for whole-grain options (corn or whole-wheat). Just as with bread, whole-grain tortillas provide more fiber and a more complete package of nutrients and health-protecting plant compounds. When buying flour tortillas, look for those made with vegetable oils."

VEGAN MEATBALLS
Algurie Wilson

Ingredients:
2 packages vegan meatballs
½ large red onion, chopped
3 to 4 garlic cloves, chopped
1 jar pasta sauce

1 teaspoon spices (dried sage, dried dill, garlic powder, salt and pepper)
Drizzle of roasted garlic extra virgin olive oil

White cheese of choice (feta, goat, mozzarella, vegan, or similar)

Combine all ingredients in a baking or roasting dish with a lid. Cover and bake for 25–30 minutes at 350°F to 400°F. Remove from oven, sprinkle with cheese and serve.

Algurie Wilson retired from the Raytheon Company and is the President Coalition for African American Health and Wellness. She. She and her husband Bernard served as former officers and presidents of the Afro-American Historical and Genealogical Society-Tucson Chapter. She says, "For some reason I put a lot of weight on because they were bringing in a lot of food in at work. Then I got here (to Tucson) and I was still obese and my doctor look at me and said, 'You know something, I might probably start putting you on diabetes medicine. You know your health is going to start going the wrong directions.' I don't know what it was about her and when she said those words, but it woke me up. I started learning how to eat. I have been eating healthy for a long time now. Because I have high blood pressure, I don't eat salt. If you put salt in your food, I will know it right away. I try to eat baked chicken, fish, I like turkey legs and I boil them twice to boil the salt out of them. I eat wheat pasta, salads, I do fruits. I haven't been to a fast-food restaurant in I don't know how long. And if I have to go, I will try to get the healthiest things they have. I look at salt, fat and if the healthiest thing they have is a parfait, then that's what I get. I stay away from processed food. I like eating healthy. This recipe is from my daughter."

Editor's note: Vegan, garden-based meatballs are available in many stores, from Walmart to Trader Joe's.

BC'S SPECIAL BAKED CHICKEN
Bryan Carter. Ph.D.

Ingredients:
4 large boneless skinless chicken breasts
1 can of cream of chicken soup
Chopped onion
Chopped celery
Pinch of Lawry's seasoned salt
Pinch of poultry seasoning
2 potatoes, peeled and cubed
1 tablespoon of butter

Thaw chicken and rinse. Place in an oven safe dish. Pour cream of chicken soup over chicken. Sprinkle onion and celery over chicken. Add a pinch of Lawry's and of poultry seasoning. Scatter chopped potatoes around the chicken. Melt butter and add to sauce. Bake for 35 minutes (or until chicken reaches an internal temperature of 140°F).

Serve with vegetables and yeast rolls!!

The Military in Tucson, A Vital Force

Air Force members stationed at Davis-Monthan Air Force Base in Tucson during a 2020 Black History Month event. Photo by Airman 1st Class Jacob T. Stephens, 355th Wing Public Affairs.

Davis-Monthan Air Force Base, located in Tucson, brought African Americans from all over the nation into the area, and some became permanent residents. Like most military installations, the base observes Black History Month with events such as luncheons and speeches. In 2020, the 41st Electronic Combat Squadron celebrated by holding "a Black heritage flight in honor of all Black service members—past and present." Air Force descriptions of the event quote Senior Airman Jada Roth, an Arabic language analyst, as saying "We went over heritage and history, we also had personal stories that were shared with the group. We were just trying to highlight Black service members and how far we've come and how far we still have to go."

Similarly, the Fort Huachuca Army post located in the city of Sierra Vista, Arizona, has hosted Black History Month events to recognize its Black history and soldiers. Although Sierra Vista is about an hour's drive southeast of Tucson, many of its Black residents made and are still making connections with Tucson's larger Black community. The explanation lies in the opportunity to connect with national and local social and religious African American organizations as well as with cultural events in the larger city.

A Black Military presence in attendance at a Fort Huachuca event circa 1943. These were members of the Ninth Service Command. Marguerite Euell Sanchez collection.

As of 2020, Black people made up 7.7 percent of Sierra Vista's population of 45,308, while Tucson's Black population stands at 5.2 percent of 542,62. Since 1892, when Buffalo Soldiers and other segregated Black regiments were stationed at Fort Huachuca, trips to Tucson were not uncommon and happened for identical reasons—the desire to be with people who share cultural perspectives, practices and experiences at key moments.

The first Black soldiers became scouts and bilingual interpreters, often working alongside American Indians in the same occupations. Some of those Black men made Arizona, and later Tucson, their home. They represented many different kinds of people. But they can be described as aggressively determined to survive and deeply aware of military prospects.

Fort Huachuca has a special history in that it served as a home for several Buffalo Soldiers units after the Civil War. The National Park Service notes that American Plains Indians gave the name Buffalo Soldiers to Black service men "because of their dark, curly hair, which resembled a buffalo's coat and because of the fierce nature of their engagements. The nickname soon became synonymous with all African-American

World War II members of the Tucson USO organization hosted events for military men stationed at Fort Huachuca and Davis Monthan Air Force Base. Marguerite Euell Sanchez collection.

SEQUENCE OF EVENTS

Invocation
SFC Keiden S. Jones

National Anthem
PFC Novelyn R. Ocampo

Opening Remarks
LTC Wendy L. Gray

Video Production

Presidential Proclamation
SGT Arthur J. Cross, III

Keynote Speaker
Dr. Tani D. Sanchez

Closing Remarks
LTC Wendy L. Gray

Dr. Tani D. Sanchez, Associate Professor, Univ. of Arizona

Dr. Sanchez is primarily interested in racial representations in the media and in the study of African American history and culture. She worked for a number of years as an editor, broadcast journalist and as a media information specialist. She is also the first president of the Tucson Chapter Afro-American Historical and Genealogical Society (founded by Gloria Smith), an active member of the Tucson Black Film Club and is a member of the Women's Progressive and Civic Club. She has served as a State President of the National Association of Colored Women's Clubs. Dr. Sanchez has a doctorate in Comparative Cultural and Literary studies; her masters degree focused on visual culture/art history while her undergraduate studies included Radio and Television.

She has lectured in Tucson and other cities on Black history, racial representations in film, and on African American family history and genealogy. Her wide-ranging background in broadcast and written journalism as well as in public affairs has included overseas assignments in the U.S. Army and a stint in the Arizona National Guard.

Her academic writings have been published in two anthologies; she has created political videos and has written and edited books and newsletters for community based associations. In addition to classes in Africana Studies, Dr. Sanchez has also taught art history and art appreciation courses.

regiments formed in 1866." During World War II, tens of thousands of African American enlisted men processed through Fort Huachuca on the way to other assignments. The Tucson/Fort Huachuca interactions still happen. For example, in 2021 a Black history luncheon featured soul foods and a keynote address by Tani Sanchez of the University of Arizona's Africana Studies program. Raised in Tucson, she is an Army veteran.

Another less known part of Tucson's history involves Lt. Henry O. Flipper, the first Black graduate of the United States Military Academy at West Point in 1877. While at the academy, he still made above average grades. Nonetheless, he was shunned and forced into "almost total social isolation from his classmates." Most of his military service was successful and he was eventually stationed at Fort Huachuca. In 1882, he was dishonorably discharged under problematic circumstances. It was not until almost 100 years later that "President Clinton granted a full and unconditional pardon" to Flipper for his questionable discharge. Flipper continually fought the discharge throughout his life.

However, Henry Flipper has historically stood out as a "symbol of Black achievement." After his discharge, Flipper lived for a good number of years in the Grand Canyon state, becoming a "familiar figure in Tucson."

Flipper's post-military career included testimony in a Tucson court room after conducting a property survey that involving the town of Nogales. Arizona history writer Jane Eppinga reported, "A headline in the Oasis, another Nogales newspaper, proclaimed 'Long Live Flipper!'"

An article originally published in The Journal of Arizona History says he "spent much of the 1890s in southern Arizona, where he surveyed the Nogales townsite, briefly edited a local newspaper, and defended the community in an important land grant case. As special agent to the Court of Private Land Claims, he saved over 700,000 acres from falling into the hands of unscrupulous speculators. Remarkably, his important contributions to Arizona history are all but forgotten today."

Cadet Henry Flipper.

In 2022, West Point recognized his perseverance and life by granting Cadet Zorian Flowers the *Henry O. Flipper Award* for overcoming hardship.

As a larger historical note in this military section, involvement of Blacks in American military actions and patriotic conflicts occurred not just after the Civil War, but much earlier, even before and during the Revolutionary War of 1775. Many people know the story of Crispus Attucks, killed first during the 1770 Boston Massacre skirmish with British forces. But others also became involved. For them, freedom issues in a slavocracy had different faces. Like Attucks, some had interest in the national conflict although many whites, including George Washington, initially opposed arming and training either free or enslaved Blacks. But as the war wore on and forces depleted, Maj. Glenn Williams, a historian at the U.S. Army Center for Military History, writes that approval came and "most historians believe that 10 to 15 percent" of the American revolutionary force was Black. Some colonial legislatures promised freedom for service. Heroic, compelling stories of heroism survive. In other cases, Blacks were forced to fight by slave owners and never received compensation. Other Blacks considered the issues of tyranny from another aspect, choosing to fight for the British who also offered release from slavery.

During the Civil War, 179,000 Blacks served as soldiers of the United States Colored Troops. They knew the freedom and lives of millions of African Americans were at stake and they stepped up. Others, male and female, served as spies who passed critical information from inside Confederate homes to the Union, or were cooks, washer women, or worked in other areas of support.

Arizona and Tucson are important locations in the greater story of African Americans in military careers.

Interviews about Contemporary Military Life

Debi Chess: I'm a military brat. I grew up in the Air Force. My father was in the Air Force, and so I mostly grew up on military bases, and then my father retired at Wright-Patterson Air Force Base in Dayton, Ohio, so that's where I found myself going to junior high school, high school, and even college. I went to Wright State University. We landed there because my father was in the Air Force.

I'm so glad you asked this question because a lot of Tucson feels like Fairborn, Ohio, where the military base was where I grew up, where the Black folks that you interacted with were so transient because you'd be here for a year, or two years, or three years at the max, and then you'd move on. So, I was the only Black child in my elementary school. Then, when I got to junior high and high school, there were more Black kids, but it was because of the military base. But again, it was very transient. A few were like mine, their parents retired and so their family stayed like my family did.

The military had a huge impact on my life, and the informing of my Blackness as well, because we lived in predominantly white neighborhoods and it was my parents' insistence that we went to Black churches, we were involved in "Jack and Jill." My parents had purposely cultivated a Black community for us, just like I've had to cultivate my Black community here in Tucson. You would think that that would be so evident to me, but it hasn't been until you asked that question. Sometimes I reflect back on it and I think "Oh, my gosh." I'll have this internal feeling or this feeling of familiarity that I don't understand sometimes and I think, "Oh, that's my childhood. That's coming from my experience as a military child and a Black military child." So, when I get these déjà vu moments, this instinctual feeling that something seems so familiar, it's because of that.

Sadie Shaw: My grandpa, along with my dad and my uncle, moved to Tucson from East St. Louis where my dad was born. I have heard several different accounts from family members. The reason was the opportunity in Arizona. Not as racist as a place. He didn't want his sons and daughters to be called the N-word every day. And also, my granddad was a World War II veteran and there were a lot of military people moving here. It was a lot of people from Texas and the South.

Brena Andrews: If anything, it has been good as far as finding more Black people to connect with because a lot of the young Black people here, if they're not here for school, they're here for the military or the military family. So, it's really cool as far as bringing more Black people here so we can have some sort of community, because without them there really wouldn't be that many Black people in Tucson.

Gloria Smith: I used to research African American history in Arizona. And so, I did research the military history with the four Black regiments down at Fort Huachuca and of course the Buffalo Soldiers. I traveled around lecturing about the Buffalo Soldiers, and the topic I used was "The Buffalo Soldiers of Yesterday, Today, and Tomorrow."

Another thing I did do was explore the involvement of African Americans in the three C's of Arizona: cotton, copper, and cattle. They were involved in all three of those industries. Arizona had some of the best cotton in the world. For cattle, we had some Black ranchers that were very successful. One had a ranch of 640 acres of land in Wilcox, Arizona. Another who just died recently was Edward Keeylocko. He had Keeylocko Town, and we would go out there. They often held Black rodeos out there. Not to mention the rodeo riders. Charlie Sampson was here, and Bill Pickett had also been here. He's a bulldogger who would grab the horns of a steer and twist them around and then bite him in the mouth. The cattle, the cotton … we had people who were involved in the copper industry too. They kind of had one foot in the cattle industry and one foot in the copper industry, and so African Americans were involved there. Now back to the cotton: Yuma, Arizona. It was another area of Arizona, and they were like Black cotton towns. Usually, the men had gone out to work and the ladies were left to work there. Randolph, Arizona, was one place like that.

Algurie Wilson: I can tell you a lot of stories on that. I am glad the bases are there because we have the Raytheon Missile Systems sitting there. When 9/11 happened, they had to take the F-16 up in the air a couple times to protect that base. That base is scary at the same time, because if they come to hit something, they are strategically going to hit those kinds of places. But at the same time, I felt good, because I used to work at Raytheon, so when I found out that the F-16 had to take to the air to protect the Raytheon site, it made me feel good.

I have been living here almost twenty-something years and I had a nephew that got stationed there. And when I got the call that he was going to be stationed in the next couple of days, I helped because he was going to put some stuff in the storage unit. I went to secure the keys and everything for them so when they came after hours, they were able to move in. So now I have my nephew here, because it was just me and my husband when my daughter left.

I am proud knowing that the base is there and that my nephew is there and that they decided to stay and buy a house. I am excited that I have family now. Having the base there is important; it is important for our time. If they close the base it would dry up the east side of town. The base is important to the economy and the safety of Raytheon.

Interviews about Military Life 1990s and Before

Felix Goodwin: I came in 1939 to join the Army. We obtained weekend passes to Tucson and congregated on Meyer Street. The Elks and Beehive Club were across from Mrs. Johnson's rooming house. I worked for a place to sleep and sat on benches in front of the train station watching trains, playing cards and checkers. The Blue Moon was located outside the gate at Fort Huachuca. Everyone went there to dance. Gals came over and men went across the border in Nogales to be with the girls. The Deltas (a Black sorority) came down to put on a show in the spring of 1940.

Constance Smith: USO recreation, places to go, employment.

Dr. Laura Nobles Banks-Reed: The military afforded me with the opportunity to meet a lot of interesting people and a great deal of fun, socially. I was president of the USO hostess club and helped entertain servicemen.

Anonymous 1993: I worked as a cook's help at Davis-Monthan Air Force Base. Geraldine Taylor was our head cook. We were getting 41 cents an hour. That was in 1942, and it was supposed to be civil service.

Blanche Lucille Lewis: The military and its bases gave us somewhere to go, especially when the USO was in bloom.

Marguerite Euell Sanchez: The USO brought in a place where the military could feel at home and programs and recreation and travel to bases with USO hostesses brought dances, entertainment, etc. Servicemen attended churches, and there were always weekend visitors to our home. No shortage of dates.

Have There Been Influences from Africa?

Algurie Wilson: In many ways, sometimes, yeah. I have a good friend from Ethiopia, and she was the first person that I had an interface with that came from Africa. I was involved with Girl Scouts and she would bring food and talk about how they would eat with their hands, and I learned a lot from her and understanding the types of foods. We eat squash and we eat yams and it is similar to the types of food they eat.

Petra Robertson:I have a friend; she's kind of like family. I used to work in her restaurant when I was a teenager, and I learned how to cook African and Indian food from her. She's from Africa, but she's Indian. She's from Botswana. So, I learned how to make them. Most of the foods she knew were vegetarian, so I learned how to make the Indian food and make it good enough that you didn't miss the meat. So, there are times where I can do vegetarian meals and people enjoy them. Then I put my spin on them and put meat in some of them, and they enjoy that.

Eric Oum: Most definitely. As someone who was born and raised in Cameroon, I am especially influenced by the food and cuisine from my motherland. Our traditional flavors and spices are unique to us and unrivaled by anything else. I would even go further to say that most foods—whether from America, Europe, or Asia—can be traced back to their African origins. Empanadas are a great example of this; despite being typically considered as Latin American, empanadas or meat pies can be found all around parts of western and sub-Saharan Africa. It's a great testament to how interconnected we all are, so I take pride and joy in including part of my heritage into the food I eat.

Anonymous 2021: Much of my food choices and preparations have nothing to do with my interactions with the African community in Tucson. My choice of African staples, like yams, plantains, red beans, garri [a flour made from cassava], rice, palm nut paste (for soup), groundnut paste (for soup), etc., are based on my experiences with these foods growing up in Africa. It helped that there are African/Middle Eastern shops in Tucson that sell these staples. The one big choice (pre-pandemic) that I have added to my food menu is the injera food from Ethiopia. The injera is a nutritious pancake-type flatbread that is eaten with stir-fried vegetables.

Yvonne Gathers: Back in 2008, 2010, my elderly aunt lived with me and I had to hire individuals to come and care for her while I was working. One was a young woman from Nigeria. Her cooking really impressed me. She would do shrimp and eggs. That was so good! She does something called yellow rice, and every year we would have our church group in our home, and she would always make that as one of the dishes that I would serve. One with the black-eyed peas, corn, and shrimp together. That was an African dish. It was delicious! So, the lady that I work with, the owner; the owner, she is from Cameroon. What does she eat? She hasn't really made a Cameroonian dish, but she makes a mean red rice! I don't know why it tastes so good! It's not jollof rice; no, it's regular red rice like I would make. It's really good. Shay, who is from Nigeria, has cooked for us. Even now, she'll come by with a pot of something. Several of my staff members, one woman is from Togo and most of them are from Cameroon.

Brenda Edmontson: When I was looking for a nice diet, because I read a lot. I know you've probably heard of "eat with your ancestors," which is kind of silly because when you come to think of it, we've been in the United States for 400 years or so when the first slave was brought over. We've adapted, we've intermingled, so you can't just eat African food or you can't just cook African food, because that's ridiculous. Because you have to first of all eat for who you are, because what I might be eating might make you sick but it might be helpful for me. So, I believe that you can't put a blanket over African food and say all African Americans should eat this food when we have been out of that culture for 400 years, and then to come back and reintroduce it just doesn't make sense.

Debi Chess: Not on a regular basis, but there are certainly times I've been at events. Like peanut stew. Now that the weather is changing, I'll sometimes be like "Oh, I think I'm gonna make a vegetarian peanut stew without the chicken." But it's only because I was exposed to those types of food in Chicago, and even here in Tucson through Africana Studies, through my relationship through some of those professors and events that I have gone to. So yeah, when I am cooking, I have to think about how our ancestors sustained themselves without meat. There wasn't a lot of meat available on a regular basis, and so I often think about it. It's like, if they could live without these certain lifestyles then I certainly can. Even things like I was forced to drink, understanding that I have a milk intolerance that's genetic, and not knowing that as a child, if you're still being forced to drink milk …. I guess it's a long way of saying yes. In some regards I do; that has shaped my food choices and how I prepare food.

Recipes: Meat-Based Meals

Editor's note: Many contemporary contributors for the cookbook did not emphasize beef or other meats in their recipes and diets. Some used the same recipes as before but substituted meat products, such as the recipe for vegan spaghetti and meat balls. So, is it okay to eat meat? Harvard Medical School does not say meat cannot be part of a healthy diet, but says instead that going vegetarian can lead to "lower body mass index and blood pressure; reduced risks for heart disease, diabetes, and cancer; and longer life." If you want to adjust the amount of meat in your diet, they identify several approaches: semi-vegetarian (some select meats); pescatarian (fish and seafood only); lacto-ovo vegetarian (dairy and eggs); and vegan (plant-based only).

CHILI
Brenda Edmontson
Photo by Brenda
This is a low-sodium recipe, you may want to add a teaspoon of sea salt or more, to taste.
Prep time: 30–35 minutes. Cook time: 30 minutes. Yield: 8 servings.

Brenda Edmontson is a business owner who helps other business owners stay top of mind with their clients by teaching strategies for reaching out to clients in a meaningful way. She says her recipe "started out as a vegetarian recipe. It was made from scratch and everything that's in it was either organic with nothing is from a can. It starts out with five beefsteak tomatoes and makes a really good pot. There are different seasonings and things in it. I will admit that I took it from a cookbook, but I doctored it

up and made it mine. It's no longer a vegetarian recipe; it is now a meat-based recipe. I have used bison in it and I have used 97 percent grass-fed beef, and the spices that goes in it are what makes it different."

Ingredients:

1 pound lean (80 to 85 percent ground beef (grass-fed preferred)
1 teaspoon dried oregano
½ teaspoon onion powder
½ teaspoon sea salt
¼ teaspoon black pepper
2 tablespoons sesame oil
1 large red bell pepper, chopped
1 large green bell pepper, chopped
1 large onion, chopped
2 cloves garlic, minced
5 large tomatoes, chopped

3 tablespoons low-sodium tamari
2 teaspoon cumin
1 teaspoon ginger
1 teaspoon tarragon
1 teaspoon basil
1 teaspoon cayenne pepper (optional)
2 cups canned kidney beans, rinsed
1 cup raw corn
16 ounces tomato puree
1 small can black olives, sliced or chopped
1 to 2 tablespoons of almond butter (optional)

Sauté lean ground beef with dried oregano, onion powder, sea salt, and black pepper. In a large pudding pot [or soup pot] over medium-high heat, heat sesame oil and sauté bell peppers, onion and garlic until peppers are limp. Stir in tomatoes until well combined. Add tamari, cumin, ginger, tarragon, basil and cayenne pepper (if using).

Bring to a simmer and cook over medium-high heat for about 5 minutes. Add beans, corn, tomato puree, and black olives. For an earthy flavor, add 1 to 2 tablespoons of almond butter (optional).   Combine ingredients thoroughly and reduce heat to medium-low. Simmer for at least 30 minutes, stirring occasionally. Serve with corn bread.

HOMEMADE CHILI
Hosea Johnson
This chili mixture is condensed and designed for freezer storage. This recipe can be doubled.

Ingredients:

5 pounds coarsely ground chuck or any chili meat, cooked
46 ounces tomato juice or sauce
12 ounces tomato paste
4 medium onions, chopped
4 ounces salted cracker crumbs

½ cup of chili powder
½ cup of mashed cumin seed or powdered cumin
¼ ounces crushed red pepper
1 whole clove garlic
salt and pepper to taste

Place meat in roasting pan and cook in oven at 400°F, stirring until brown. (You can also do this on the stovetop.) After meat is brown, add all remaining ingredients and use cracker crumbs to thicken. Reduce oven temperature to 350°F and cook for 1½ to 2½ hours, stirring often. Freeze in loaf pan or other container until ready to use. Will keep in the freezer for 1 year.

When ready to use, defrost and add water. Do not add water until ready to use.

OXTAILS AND BUTTER BEANS
Catherine White Mize

Ingredients:

Butter beans

Oxtails

Onion, chopped

Salt and pepper to taste

Soak beans overnight. Cook in the same water for about 30 minutes. Add oxtails, chopped onion, and seasoning. Cook slowly until done.

SPAGHETTI CASSEROLE
Norma Watson

Norma Watson taught in Tucson schools for over 40 years and was engaged in many social and professional organizations. Serves 6–8.

Ingredients:

1½ pounds ground beef

1 medium onion, diced

1 8-ounce can sliced chili peppers

1 6-ounce can Ortega green chiles

4 teaspoons ground oregano

1 teaspoon minced garlic

29 ounces Italian-style stewed tomatoes

16 ounces tomato sauce

mushrooms

salt and pepper to taste

8 ounces uncooked spaghetti

2 tablespoons Parmesan cheese

Brown ground beef in a large skillet. Remove excess fat. Add onion, chilis, oregano, and garlic. Cook over medium heat until onions are lightly browned, stirring often. Add stewed tomatoes, tomato sauce, and mushrooms. Salt and pepper to taste.

Cook spaghetti following package directions. Drain and rinse with hot water. Combine cooked spaghetti and meat mixture in a large casserole dish. Sprinkle Parmesan cheese on top and bake at 350°F for 30–35 minutes.

EGUSI SOUP
Bosede Ijagbemi

Originally from Nigeria, Bosede currently works as a nurse in a local hospital. Active in the local Nigerian community, she says, "Our food is really nutritious. We tend to keep with our African culture. [We] have mainly African food to eat, drink." She also says, "Egusi is the name for the fat-and protein-rich seed consumed in Nigeria, West Africa."

Ingredients:
3 cups egusi (dried, ground melon seeds)
1 medium stockfish
4 smoke-dried fish
4.4 pounds goat meat (optional)   Vegetables
4.4 pounds cow legs (optional)   Oil for cooking
Onion, chopped or sliced
Seasonings

Wash meat, season to taste on the stove and cook for 10 minutes. Put the stockfish on the stove and cook for 30 minutes, as this takes longer; cook it until it's soft. Heat oil on the stove in a separate pot, mix the egusi with water and add to the oil. Add onion and a little water at a time and simmer for 10 minutes. Season to taste. Add meat, smoke-dried fish, and stockfish and cook for 20 minutes. Wash and add vegetable of choice and take off the stove. Allow to cool, and serve.

Editor's note: Stockfish is dried unsalted whitefish, such as cod. Online sources further explain that Egusi is a gourd that resembles watermelon. Seeds from the melon are ground and used for cooking Nigerian and other West African soups. It is said to taste nutty and spicy, and can be purchased at Tucson's Nur Market & Restaurant at 3565 E. Speedway, #171, or online at nur-market.square.site. Pumpkin seeds are sometimes substituted for egusi in the U.S. Some recipes add tomatoes and stock. Several times I would go to my Africana Studies office at the University of Arizona, located next to that of my colleague Dr. Bayo Ijagbemi. At lunch time, delicious smelling foods made by his wife Bosede would emanate.

CAMEROONIAN NDOLÉ
Eric Oum
Photo by Eric Oum

Ingredients:
½ pounds of stew beef
1 large onion, sliced, divided in half portions
1 bouillon cube (Maggi)
½ pounds of stockfish (Bifaga)
2 cups of peanuts (skinless)
1 cup water
4 to 5 cloves of garlic
¾ cup crayfish
1 pound frozen spinach
½ pounds of shrimp
5 to 7 plantains (boiled or fried)
oil for cooking

In a large pan, boil the stew beef with half of the sliced onions and Maggi until the meat is tender. Meanwhile, in another pot, boil the stockfish with salt and water until tender. Add the stockfish to the stew beef.

Boil peanuts for about 10 minutes, then blend the peanuts in a mixer with about 1 cup of water. Add the peanut mixture to the meat and stockfish.

Blend remaining 1/2 onion with garlic and add it to the pot. Pour crayfish in the pot and let it simmer for 10 minutes. Season with salt and Maggi. Stir.

Add the spinach to the pan. Stir and simmer for several more minutes. Sauté shrimp. Add the sautéed shrimp and serve hot with a side of plantain!

Eric Oum is originally from Cameroon. He says, "Since the pandemic I have made sure that everything I eat in a day serves a purpose for whatever tasks I may have to do that day. A banana may be burned while climbing a few flights of stairs later, or if I eat a heavier meal that day, I may plan some late-night pool cleaning. It all depends on my daily schedule—which makes this style of eating more freeing."

Eric Oum

TANI'S SPICY BAR-B-QUE RIBS
Tani Sanchez

Ingredients:
⅓ cup Louisiana Hot Sauce
Barbecue sauce
½ cup Worcestershire sauce

Beef short ribs (English/flanken cut)
Seasoned salt, *or* creole seasoning

Mix sauces and place in a shallow dish. Marinate ribs an hour or so, turning once. Remove ribs and sprinkle heavily with seasoned salt. Roast slowly over an open flame or broil in the oven. Drain fat from the ribs. Add generous amounts of your favorite barbecue sauce and grill or roast just enough to get a crispy singe.

You can also throw these in an Instant Pot and cook until tender—15 minutes or so. Place on foil, brush with barbecue sauce, and then broil in the oven until the top is crisp but not burnt. Turn if desired. Watch them constantly as you broil or cook on the grill.

SAM'S COUNTRY RIBS
Eunice Rhodes
Serves 4.

Ingredients:

4 pounds country-style ribs
Garlic salt to taste
1½ cups barbecue sauce

½ bunch scallions or green onions, sliced
1 bunch fresh parsley, rinsed and dried, to garnish

Sprinkle ribs on both sides with garlic salt. Place in a shallow pan. Combine the barbecue sauce and scallions and pour over ribs. Cover and marinate at room temperature for 2 hours. Pour off most of the marinade and reserve. Bake the ribs, uncovered, for 1 hour in an oven preheated to 350°F. Pour off juices and place ribs under broiler or on grill. Use reserved marinade to baste ribs. Broil or grill 5 minutes. Served garnished with parsley.

Editor's note: Eunice and her husband Sam moved to Tucson two decades ago. They lived in Chicago before relocating, where Samuel Rhodes attended culinary school, worked as a chef, and eventually owned his own restaurant. He is now deceased, but Eunice shares his recipes and is sharing his culinary tradition as she transitions from medical supervisory fields to the hospitality industry.

LOVE 'EM OR LEAVE 'EM CHITLINS SHISH KEBABS
Gloria Smith

Ingredients:
1 small bucket of pork chitterlings   Vinegar
Louisiana hot sauce

Thaw chitterlings, clean carefully, and boil in the traditional fashion (about 2 hours in water and vinegar, adding water as needed). When done, drain. Place long chitterlings on foot-long skewers. Pierce them with a fork, sprinkle with hot sauce and broil. Watch carefully and remove when almost crisp. Serve warm with potato salad.

Gloria Smith came to Tucson in the 1970s. A retired research librarian at the University of Arizona and former Black Studies coordinator, she is one of the charter members of the national Afro-American Historical and Genealogical Society, as well a founder of the former Arizona and Tucson chapters. She created this recipe in Massachusetts when she got a new stove. "Some people in the family like chitlins and some people don't. I got a new stove that has a grill at the top, so I decided I'm gonna first cook the chitlins, then I'm gonna put them on skewers. Then I'm gonna pierce them with a fork and put some Louisiana Hot Sauce on them, and some ketchup on the others, and I'm gonna grill to get some of the grease out of them. I took them to a church soul food dinner that we had. I laid them on the table, and this one kid came by. My kid was there, and his friend was there with him. His friend said, 'What are those?' My kid turned around and said, 'If you don't know what they are, leave them alone.' So that's why I came up with the Love 'Em or Leave 'Em Chitlin Shish Kebobs.

"Chitlins were something that we enjoyed. It was a celebration. You could buy a bucket of chitlins for ten dollars, and you could just cook them. My mother fried them. She decided to be different, so I decided I'm gonna be different; I'm gonna grill them! So, my chitlins shish kebobs are called Love 'Em or Leave 'Em Chitlins Shish Kebobs because if you don't know what they are, don't bother with them. We'd be very upset if you waste chitlins. Fights have broken out in the ghetto over people going in and so 'Ooooh, what's that?' filling up their plate and not eating them. That's so much that the other people could have been eating if you hadn't wasted them. So, my son had the right idea when he told his pal 'If you don't know what they are, leave them alone.'

Editor's note: Ever heard of tricandilles or andouillette? Chitterlings are prepared, served, and loved in countries all over the world, with diverse recipes from Japan to France to the United Kingdom. In soups, floured and fried, or ground up in sausages, the intestines can come from cows, goats, or lamb. The Centers for Disease Control says, "If you choose to prepare raw chitlins, you can take steps to protect children and other people in your house from germs that can spread around the kitchen and to people. The most important step in preventing

Grilled chitterlings sold on the street in Thailand

infection is handwashing. While preparing raw chitlins, be sure to wash your hands thoroughly before you touch children and things they may touch or put in their mouths, including toys, pacifiers, bottles, and food. You'll need to take other actions, too, to prevent spreading germs from raw chitlins."

FRIED SCRAPPLE
Pecolia L. Hayes and Gloria Smith

Ingredients:
Philadelphia scrapple (in a can or from a butcher)
Flour
Hot oil

Slice scrapple into ½"-thick pieces. Roll each slice in flour and fry in hot oil. Serve with eggs for breakfast. This can be served with hominy grits.

Editor's note: Scrapple is associated with the Pennsylvania Dutch people, but it is eaten in other regions. Scrapple can include trimmings, such as the skin, head, heart, and liver. These usually come from pork or, in contemporary times, turkey. The scrapple is mixed with cornmeal and syrup, then formed into a loaf. Seasoned and ready to go, it can be purchased commercially or made at home. Scrapple is not Spam, which has no organ meat, but the principle is similar.

SPAGHETTI SAUCE WITH MEATBALLS
John Ross

Ingredients:
3 pounds ground beef
6 eggs
2 tablespoons green seasoning (green ground beef seasoning blend)
6 to 8 slices of bread, torn into pieces and soaked in milk

dried oregano, to taste
2 large cans tomato sauce
basil flakes (for sauce)
salt, onion salt, and parsley to taste
1 (12 ounce) can tomato paste

Mix ground beef, eggs, green seasoning, milk-soaked bread, and oregano until well combined. Roll into meatballs. Put tomato sauce, basil, salt, onion salt, and parsley in a large pan or pressure cooker. Brown (fry) the meatballs in a large skillet. Drain grease and add meatballs to sauce. In the same skillet, add tomato paste and 2½ cans of water. Simmer for 15 minutes to reduce, then add to the sauce. Pressure cook for 30 minutes, or simmer in a large pot or pan for 2 hours.

Editor's note: I was never really sure what green seasoning meant, but Jamillia Joseph, former Tucson restaurant owner, describes green seasoning as "a blend of fresh seasonings and herbs. Some examples are onions, green peppers, garlic, and thyme. The list can go on depending on what you want."

HAM TETRAZZINI
Hearon Hayes

Ingredients:

6 pounds ham
2½ pounds elbow macaroni
1 pound butter
2 cups of flour
½ teaspoon pepper

1 teaspoon ground marjoram
1 gallon milk
¾ pound cheese, grated
1 (7 ounce) jar of diced pimentos

Dice ham into ½-inch pieces. Cook macaroni according to directions, with salt. Melt butter in the top of a double boiler, then add flour, pepper, and ground marjoram. Blend until smooth. Add milk, stirring constantly until thickened. Cover and cook 10–15 minutes or until there is no "starchy" flavor. Add grated cheese and stir until melted. Stir in pimentos and diced ham. Fold in macaroni. Pour into 2 greased 20¾″ × 12¾″ × 2½″ pans and bake in slow oven (325°F) for 30–40 minutes.

BAKED BRISKET ROAST
Ethel M. Quattlebaum

Ingredients:

4-pound brisket roast
1 cup ketchup
1 cup water
1 tablespoon prepared mustard
1 tablespoon fresh chopped onion

1 tablespoon horseradish
1 tablespoon vinegar
2 teaspoons salt
¼ teaspoon pepper

Combine ketchup, water, onion, vinegar, mustard, horseradish, salt and pepper. Pour over brisket. Cover and refrigerate overnight. Preheat oven to 300°F. Bake 4 hours.

Ethel M. Quattlebaum was a faithful member of Prince Chapel A.M.E church and traveled extensively with her husband James.

NECKBONES
Irene T. Hutcherson

Ingredients:

Neckbones (beef, pork, turkey)
1 medium onion, cut in quarters
2 stalks of celery, sliced ¼-inch thick

Salt and pepper to taste
1 clove garlic

Cook neckbones and onions in water with celery, salt, pepper and garlic until tender. Make a paste with ¼ cup of fine flour and water. Pour in the pot to thicken for gravy. This dish may be poured over pasta or rice. Have several napkins available to enjoy the meat sufficiently.

Editor's note: A special education teacher, Irene T. Hutcherson was actively involved in the YWCA, Up with People, and the Alpha Kappa Alpha Sorority, the first such intercollegiate historically African American group. A board member of the National Association for the Advancement of Colored People, a past president of the Tucson Chapter of The Links, incorporated, her interests included educational, civic and inter-cultural activities.

HAM BONES AND BUTTER BEANS
Anonymous 1993

Ingredients:

½ cup pinto [or butter] beans

1 ham bone

8 to 10 cups cold water

½ cup chopped onions

½ cup chopped red bell pepper

¼ cup chopped garlic

Red (cayenne) pepper to taste

Salt and black pepper to taste

Wash beans and pick out any that are not good. Put beans, ham bone, and the rest of the ingredients in a pot. Start cooking on hot fire. After it begins to boil, cook at low to medium heat until most of the water has cooked out. Sample a bean by mashing to see if they are done. It usually takes between 30 minutes and 2 hours.

Entertainment, Social and Civic Life

Since 2012, the Tucson Black Film Club has screened movies several times a year and hosted an annual Film festival. Normally held at the Dunbar Pavilion, the events are currently virtual. They explain, "As film or movie enthusiast we are in a unique position to examine and explore the evolution of film, the evolution of visual images and roles, and the cultural and social impact of film as we share and enjoy this experience with the community." Members pictured in the above right image include, from left to right, Barbara Lewis, Shirley Hockett, Annie Sykes, Debi Chess and Tani Sanchez. Annie Sykes is a leader in the Black Film Club and in the Black Women's Task Force. Shirley Hockett is a travel consultant and owner of Arizona Travel Tips, and a board member of The Dunbar Coalition, Inc.

These Elks from Phoenix, Tucson and California circa 1950s met often for charitable works and socializing among friends. Although denied membership in Tucson's white Elks clubs, the African American associations proliferated after the Civil War and arguably tie into society membership societies endemic in Western African cultures before colonialism. Photo from the Marguerite Euell Sanchez collection.

What makes life sweet? Love and the interactions with people we with care for. Think picnics, church dinners, dances, joyful music with bands and soulful singers. Think special occasions, swanky parties, trips to eating establishments, and watching movies with friends. Sitting on the porch talking to family members. Visits from beloved persons in our social networks. The sounds of children at birthday parties. All of these occur in Black communities. Professor Cornell West writes that it is culture that energized Blacks and served as a vehicle for both fighting off nihilism and indoctrination, even in the worst of times. Black interaction has been a source of love and joy.

Being Black in Tucson often means being at the very least bicultural. It means the ability to interact and mix with other races and ethnic groups while enjoying your own. The interaction may be flavored with overt or subtle biases and misinformation, but the key to understanding what is imposed by negative outside sources versus what is actually real can be linked to Black oral history, Black subjugated knowledges and Black community. As Cornel West theorizes, this cultural impetus is essential for survival and for the activism that betters life for all people. Film director Spike Lee offered his take on this matter of understanding in his 2000 film *Bamboozled*. In the film, Blacks knowingly and unknowingly absorbed or resisted the racist culture's irrational beliefs and behaviors. *Bamboozled* also addressed the issue of Black

Juneteenth Mobility Morning

REID PARK | JUNE 19TH | 8AM -- 9AM

In celebration of Juneteenth, join us for a 2 mile mobility morning. Roll, walk, run, ride, whatever gets you around, let's get around Reid Park! We will be meeting at the Cancer Memorial.

APORTELA

Andres A. Portela, a Board member of the Tucson Urban League, created and sponsored this event. He says the activity reflects his pride in his African American heritage and community. Image used with his permission.

cultural appropriation when the adoption of "Black" culture does not reflect an awareness nor an appreciation for Blackness at its most basic human core — as intelligent, positive affirming, loving existences of a particular people, their history, culture, or even its cuisines. The trick to grounding is to consciously plan for authentic Black experiences rather than the stereotypes and supremacy myths presented as true and common knowledge.

The myths? Blacks cannot succeed, that they are morally deviant, they have no ability to critique or strategize and have not been doing this for years under the most trying circumstances. Other myths are that extreme joy cannot exist in being Black or that there is no heroic past. Like-minded souls celebrate in local assemblies, in Listservs receiving news notices, announcements of performances, local events, current happenings, and lectures you will certainly otherwise miss. Black groups can be found on Facebook. There is even one named Being Black in Tucson, AZ. It won't necessarily be easy getting plugged in, but it is possible. The Tucson experience may be different, but it can include Blackness as understood by many.

Barbea Williams, director of the Barbea Williams Performing Company.

As in the past, small and large clubs, groups, and other organizations exist. Some are part of national entities that have been around for a century or more. These include the Women's Progressive and Civic Club (part of the National Association of Colored Women's Clubs), the National Urban League, and the NAACP. Others are part of churches, women's and men's service groups, or choirs. Some are political—the Pima County African American Democratic Caucus comes to mind. Others have an academic influence or origin, such as the high school African American culture clubs, the Black Law Student's Association, the fraternities and sororities, the University of Arizona Black Alumni, Alpha Phi Alpha fraternity, Delta Sigma Theta sorority, and so on. These groups sponsor balls, charity events, and other affairs such as group attendance at local theatrical performances.

Some local groups include the Black Retirees Association, Buffalo Soldiers groups, the Black Women's Task Force, and the Tucson Black Film Club. Some groups are formal or informal offshoots of larger workplaces such as Raytheon, the defense contractor and industrial corporation. Others are committees that plan and sponsor major events, such the annual Juneteenth celebrations, a celebration of the emancipation of enslaved Blacks. The Juneteenth events have ranged from a one-day to a three-day festival., Originally held at the A Mountain Park, it moved to the larger Kennedy Park for many years, and then to the Dunbar Pavilion. New celebratory events included the Harambee Festival at the Donna Liggins Center. A Black Business Expo also premiered at The Dunbar Pavilion.

The Barbea Williams Performing Company offers regular performance events and dance classes. The popular *Our Blackness, Our Heritage* step show, organized by daughter Beah Williams, attracts youthful Black participants and groups from across the city. Hundreds of Blacks residents and many vendors attend. Local rap performances and private parties in various venues are also part of the Tucson scene.

At the top of the list of grounding experiences are interactions with family members and close friends who make Blackness in everyday life tangible. Many others maintain cultural experiences by regularly *leaving* town to go to Phoenix, the much larger state capital or out of state, for events such as theatrical shows and visiting performances by major Black entertainers. For some, it is just the pleasure of seeing cities like Atlanta with miles of clean, proud, successful Black neighborhoods.

Blacks in early Tucson also worked to connect with each other. But many accounts say it was easier since there were so few Black people in town that almost "everyone knew everyone else." In 1884, the Black "Wide Awake Colored Club" sought political patronage. A later creation, the Nonpartisan Civic and Political Clubs of Pima County, developed in 1922, was able to gain jobs for African Americans and had as its goal "to improve the Negro electorate." This club, along with the NAACP and other local organizations, successfully defeated an attempt to "exclude disabled Negro veterans from the Veterans hospital on South Sixth Avenue." The Pima County Democratic Club of the late 1920s concerned itself with voting issues, maintaining that membership in both parties would "serve as an equilibrium, safeguarding the Negro in the event that either of the major parties would win an election."

The focus on "equilibrium" is not surprising. Exclusion from public facilities and from mainstream city activities was the norm. Movie theaters traditionally segregated their audiences, and in 1942 the Tucson newspaper *Arizona's Negro Journal* printed an angry story entitled "Lyric

Arizona Historical Society. Tucson Blacks in the early 1900s.

This image is from the Marguerite Euell Sanchez Collection, circa 1950s. The photo says "Sunsetters" on the back, presumably a local group. Sidney and Etta Dawson are the couple on the far right. Sidney earned a bachelor's degree from the University of Kansas and a master's degree from the University of Arizona. He taught at Dunbar in the 1940s up until integration and later became a Tucson principal, active in many organizations. He acted in movies such as "Revenge of the Nerds" and "Raising Arizona." Etta Dawson also taught at Dunbar and became a University of Arizona Black Alumni Phenomenal Woman in 1989. She was also active in many local groups.

Theatre Refuses Negro Soldiers Seats." Similar stories chronicled various incidents of eateries and stores that refused to serve African Americans and publicized employment discrimination. Issues of exclusion and rejection, despite pleasant exceptions, are still felt by many.

But of course, life is and was not always about serious issues, no matter how pressing, and this chapter is about *sweets*. Turn-of-the-century hayrides were popular. Family and friends would pack up picnic baskets, harness the horses, and go. Streetside baseball and football games attracted both young and old in the 1890s through the 1920s. One of the biggest celebrations for Tucson's African Americans was and still is held on or about June 19th. Juneteenth is the Texas-inspired holiday of emancipation. Partying groups would hitch up buggies and head "down 29th Street" to Silver Lake, before floods destroyed the artificial lake.

On Thursday and Saturday evenings, "you could see the colored people" assemble on Congress and Stone Streets. Everyone knew everyone else, and for many it was a time to get dressed and show off. One short, dark man was known for his derby hat and trim coat. He'd quip coolly, "Have you seen the governor?" There was also room for a traditional Western activity-social drinking. In early days, the Heidel Hotel and nearby saloons opened their bars to everyone regardless of race, says one resident.

Another stirring event occurred annually when the Jubilee Singers from Fisk University arrived, drawing Black and white attendees from everywhere. But, by one account, the most exciting entertainment in those days was held down in the Tucson Opera House on Congress Street; traveling minstrels would visit every year. Biannual carnivals and the Raymond Brothers circuses also sparked attendance and interest all over the Black community. Silent and sound movies played to enthusiastic African American audiences—but with limitations. Popular Black films would show one night only at the Fox theater and word would quickly spread around town to get ready for the late show, said city resident Catherine Mize. Mainstream films such as *Pinky*, *Cabin in the Sky* and *Stormy Weather* made lasting impressions.

When it got hot, African Americans, along with everyone else, swam in irrigation ditches. There were no formal pools in those earliest days, according to one account. With the building of the Elysian Groves, and later, in the 30s, the Oury Park opened with a "public" pool, paid for with tax dollars. Black residents were limited to use one day a week. The day was right before the pool was cleaned. Youths jitterbugged in the rear of Abby White's and Barbara's Bar-B-Q Pit on Anita Avenue and Speedway Boulevard. Once a month, the Riverside Ballroom on West Congress Street hosted dances. The Blue Moon Club also held Black dances and hosted performers. For more high-level entertainment, Tucson ladies joined the all-Black USO branch to become hostesses at socials. The swing and jazz years of 1930–1950 saw the appearance of groups like the Lacey Band and the Teddy Preston Band in nightclubs, both Black and white. The Elks club and the Beehive Club became the places to be.

Interviews about Contemporary Social Life

Sadie Shaw: I feel lucky enough that my family was from Sugar Hill (in Tucson). Just being part of a historic Black neighborhood, I think it helps to be and find and know where those Black faces are. My dad and his family moved into the neighborhood in the late 1950s. My dad was a volunteer at the Northwest Neighborhood Center, now known as the Donna R. Liggins Recreation Center. I would be at the park all the time. A lot of Black people from Tucson, whether they're from Sugar Hill or not, they knew that the Donna Liggins Center was one of the epicenters of Black culture and also, like, of just recreation too. It still is today, absolutely, even though the city has put up lots of barriers, increasing the prices there so that a lot of people [homeowners] were turned out. Black people still go to parks. People still go out to parks, like Mansfield.

So, I think that's important—to reside in a Black neighborhood or spend time in a Black neighborhood or a Black park. Just have a connection with the greater Black community and go to those annual events that have been happening since I was born, like Juneteenth festivals and all the other ones, like the Harambee festival. Dunbar of course is starting to be another Black cultural center, and I'm grateful for it. I think at the gem show, the African village is important. If any Black person happens to stumble on African village, it's a powerful thing to see. They definitely make things seem kind of rich. It's more about African spirituality. I still think there is a need for knowledge about that. With all that was stolen from us, knowing yourself is also contributing to the healing of people of the diaspora.

John Greenwood: I wish I knew about more of the Black cultural happenings in Tucson. My father was very involved in things, and in Tucson, and other aspects of just the community and working together, and bringing people together in general. I know mostly about things that are happening at the Dunbar center, with the Barbea Williams Performing Company, and, you know, that would be about it for me. I'm busy with my job. I'm single. Not a young guy, so I pretty much work all weekend. Come home, start all over. Trying to work around my house. I have a lady friend that I hang out with. I have other friends that I hang out with. That would be what I would know about. And you know, I read things on Facebook. I'm not a big Facebook [user] but I do read things on there. For events and social media in general.

Jamillia Joseph: It's not until now [since the pandemic] that I'm in a lot of Black groups on social media. A lot of them are mainly vegan. There are a few that are based out of Phoenix that's for Black business owners, Caribbean folks, just different little groups, but for the most part I've never really ever found anything in Tucson that was of us. And even when I did try to attend something that was supposed to be based around the culture, it was a big fail. I just didn't feel like they represented us well. The music was not ours and the lineup that they had just wasn't a good lineup of our people and though it was our people in a sense that were the vendors, to some extent, it still just wasn't. It was just there to make money in a sense, but not really represent the culture. So, I've not had much luck in Tucson at all with that. One thing I will say though if I would have to say anything: At the point where we were close enough to leaving, we did this experience the Dunbar Center. And the Dunbar Center was kind of where we started seeing a lot of our people and those folks tend to had been more along the lines of what I was used to seeing.

Eric Oum: I see a lot of Black folk volunteering at different local churches, in addition to a sizable Black volunteer population at the Boys & Girls Clubs. I am currently a student, so a lot of what I do is focused around that. I am the current president of African Americans in Life Sciences, in addition to being the reigning treasurer for the UA Chapter of the National Society of Black Engineers. I have also taken part in event planning alongside the UA Black Student Union for their celebration of Black Lives events. For me specifically, I haven't seen major differences as to how Blacks and other ethnic groups spend their time. A huge part of free time here is spent on leisure and sports. Everyone wants to be active in some way or another, so things such as soccer, hiking, and recreational league sports are quite popular here. In addition, I think a lot of Tucson folk have a shared love for the local car shows that happen across the city; it's an integral part of the culture here. Block parties and bar hopping are quite popular among younger adults as well.

Brenda Edmontson: Well, I used to go to the clubs, but a club is a club unless you're going to a very nice club, and there weren't that many in Tucson. I know the Chicago Bar closed. I was really shocked to see that. It was an okay club. And then there was another one on Speedway—I forgot what their name was—but that was when I was younger. But now that I am older, the only thing that I do is I hang out with my friends. We go to the movies; we go to dinners together. We go hiking together because that's what I like to do. So, for me, but it's basically hanging out with friends and creating relationships that matter. And I'm discovering that for me it's mostly not African Americans because there are just not that many. The ones that I do hang out with go to church and they are about my age, and so we go places together and things like that. As far as the entertainment there's not a lot. I love the theater and I go to the U of A because they have the theater there.

Bryan Carter: I guess I would say it's a bit disjointed from my own perspective, only because I have only been here for eight or nine years and because I don't live necessarily near many Black people. The only interaction I have with most Black people are at my church or at the university. Because I don't know very many people in the community other than those locations, it's difficult to find "community," and because, you know, we are all disbursed everywhere, I don't see there as being a Black community. I'm sure there is one, maybe around Dunbar, but everyplace seems so integrated now. It's difficult maybe to find the Black community here. So, I love going to events, such as some of the events at Reid Park, whether it be a Martin Luther King Day or a Juneteenth or something like that, or even things happening at the Dunbar Center. And it's amazing seeing a whole bunch of Black folks in the same place at one time. But other than that, it's been sparse for me.

Edria Johnson: Entertainment is lacking. You have the occasional jazz sets, that kind of thing. I don't think there's a real serious venue. They started the Hush Social Club and then they closed it because of the pandemic. They're trying to start it back up again, with the poetry readings and those kinds of things. When

I first moved here, they had four or five Black nightclubs—the Beau, four or five nightclubs—and now there aren't any that actually have a venue that's Black. If they're going to hold anything, it's usually at the Dunbar. And also, the Black Film Club that the Dunbar has. There isn't a whole lot. My girlfriend came from Atlanta. She said, "What's going on?" So, I was counting stuff out on my hand. She looked at me and said, "That's a shame. A big city like this and you can count the [Black] events on your hand."

Algurie Wilson: Do we have a Black life in Tucson, and I missed it? When I think of the Black life, I think of the connectivity that we have with people. I was raised primarily around Black people because I used to live in Los Angeles, but I have never been the person to judge a person by the skin color. Just like Martin Luther King was preaching. My thing is, unless you are in an organization or church, you don't see Black people. When I first got here, if I saw a Black person, I would get excited. I was like, wow.

Like genealogy, my husband is in the genealogy club, which is primarily African Americans; we research our ancestors. So therefore, I got involved supporting my husband. I became the president, and that's where I met Tani. I became the conference leader of the International Black Summit, where we put three different genealogy summits together, one in 2009, 2012, and 2016, in different cities.

I am really excited about it because now there is a focus on supporting Black businesses. I think that is so key because when I first got here, we tried to get involved and my husband got involved in this. They had the Black Chamber of Commerce, so I was all excited. I think it is so key for us to start supporting and helping each other.

Living with Coronavirus, Organizations, Changes

Tina L. Johnson: I would like to talk about the pre-COVID time. The most interesting thing about Black life in Tucson is that it is spread across Tucson. We don't congregate in one area. At some time, I think it must have been on the west side of town, downtown, but now we're all over. North, east, south, west. I found community by actually going out to the grocery store, going to the hairdresser, and one of the things I found was also attending events that were held in Tucson. And that's what makes it a big difference now.

[Since the pandemic} I can't say that I participate in a lot of the online events. It mostly consists of the Zoom, and I am ready to not participate anymore. I don't know anyone anymore. I am not on email Listservs, so I don't hear from anybody. I was with the Black Women's Task Force, the Pan Asian Community Alliance, the Board of the Stella Mann Neighborhood Association—I am the interim president of that—on the Board of the University of Arizona Black Alumni Club. I am a Delta Sigma Theta sorority member. I don't get to do anything, go anywhere. I have my son and his family, but they live in another city, Corona de Tucson, so I don't get to see them. I don't get to see my grandson, my friends' families who I used to hang out with, their kids. I don't get to see them. I don't do anything.

I've been vaccinated. I know a lot of people have not been vaccinated, so I am trying to not hang out with them. I find a lot of my friends don't want to be vaccinated. They don't. My life has been shuttered, but I have to look at the perspective. People have died. I haven't. So, I'm doing okay.

Lorna Ingram: I'm in a bubble now. I don't get to see people that I really, really miss. I mean, we can Zoom all we want, but it's not the same thing. When you do get on a Zoom, sometimes you laugh, and you miss the time that you were all together. A lot of times, the meetings we have held were our socialization and fellowship. Plus, I always liked to bring food, so we'd sit around, we do our meeting, we fellowship, and then we go home. Now we don't have that and it's pretty sad. Luckily, I've had other outlets, but I do miss my friends a lot.

Eric Oum: I have noticed that I am a lot more cautious with where and what I eat. Previously, I would try to find new restaurants and grocery stores to shop out of. However, given the public safety precautions put in place due to coronavirus, I have been hesitant to go to new businesses and local restaurants. I hope that in the future, however, the landscape to explore new food avenues will be redesigned to accommodate the current way of life.

Anonymous 2021: The pandemic has compelled me to spend more time at home with food preparation. My food choices have not changed. My shopping habits have changed, though. For example, I limit my shopping trips to one grocery where I can make bulk purchases, instead of several trips to different groceries in different parts of town. This way I limit my exposure to crowds.

Edria Johnson: I can say I scaled down. Since I didn't have anything else to do, I started growing vegetables in pots out on my patio, like a little farm. I wasn't doing that before. I have tomatoes, kale and collard greens, broccoli, and some lettuce right now. I tried to grow some potatoes. That didn't work too well, so I'm going to try that again when it gets cooler. You go to the stores and some of the vegetables are not as fresh as you want them to be. To be honest, I didn't have anything else to do. My daughter started talking about growing fresh vegetables, so it sounded like a good idea to me.

Sadie Shaw: I have definitely gotten healthier since the pandemic. Beforehand I would just eat. I try to be more conscious of what I put into my body. Looking at the World Health Organization website, I was worried for underdeveloped countries and how they would fare but it's the developed countries that are doing worse. A lot of that has to do with nutrition. The countries with the high-gluten diet are doing worse because it affects our gut, the way that we absorb nutrients. I have been trying to stay away from gluten bread, eating more fresh food and vegetables.

Gloria Smith: We aren't getting together for Thanksgiving. We will not get together for Thanksgiving dinner. That just doesn't make sense. Some people said they're gonna go outside and they're gonna do it. Sometimes, you're so happy with your little grandkids that you want to hug them. You're so happy with all the other people that you see that traveled so far to see you … that's just not gonna happen. We're just not gonna do it because it doesn't make sense. Wear your mask. Eat alone if you need to, but be happy with the fact that you're here and you're able to do that. So, Thanksgiving is something you still need to use your good sense. You really love people and you want to hug them … it's not a good idea right now.

Jamillia Joseph: It hasn't been until most recently that I have discovered Black groups on social media. A lot of them are mainly vegan. There are a few that are based out of Phoenix that are for Black business owners, Caribbean folks, and just small groups, but for the most part I've not really ever found anything in Tucson that was of us.

Brenda Edmontson: As far as the coronavirus is concerned, I think that a virus is different than a bacterium. A viral infection is usually more different to get rid of than a bacterial infection. What I try to do is I try to get my body like a repellent to a virus, and so I know that for me I just have to stay healthy, and I have to try and be as active as I possibly can. The only thing that I've actually done is I've upped my water intake. As far as health is concerned this is what I believe for myself, I believe that for me, I control a good proportion of how healthy I am. And I know that for me to be healthy I need to eat foods that are actually going to feed my body and try to get rid of all the other, like excess sugar, excess salt. So, I read labels, and the reason I do that is I don't like to be sick.

Brena Andrews: I think African Americans specifically don't have a complete culture because we were taken, but in general I feel like Black people have a big emphasis of spending time together in different ways. I know there's this idea that Black people are sort of vain or really into ourselves or being alone with technology but there's always a vibe. We are always trying to find the next move, always trying to find where to find events where we can find each other. I think there is this emphasis on hanging out with each other or being in the presence of each other; and I feel like with other groups, it's not the same. It's definitely not the same. I feel like that's just a part of America. Especially with a lot of us coming from low-income backgrounds. What is there to do? Spend time with each other and to do things. It's hard because I am not in those other cultures, but that's what I see compared to mainstream culture.

Yvonne Gathers: The pandemic has not encouraged me to make any food changes. I was thinking the other day, other than wearing a mask and limiting social engagements, the pandemic really has not impacted us that much, because we [including husband Merle] are not out. I've been concerned about the time of year this year, because I typically do get respiratory illness—pneumonia or something like that. I have been taking extra vitamins to kind of ward off. We were starting to change our eating habits before the pandemic, and that was basically because of his [my husband Merle's] illness. You know, the pandemic really has not impacted me other than Zooming. I don't like Zooming, so that's the only big change, and not being able to see my friends. We would normally get together on Thanksgiving; we didn't do that. We don't know what Christmas is going to look like. I have friends of years where we would get together and go to dinner because nobody wants to cook anymore. That's the only thing I miss.

One Man's Thoughts

John Greenwood: You know, I'd moved out of my parents' house. I thought I knew everything, and I found myself, like, I realized I was Black. After that, I knew. Now I wasn't some kid from high school, but a Black man in this community. The process was still interesting. I still was who I was. I still had the friends I had, but I now have the reality of the cultural perspective that maybe wasn't what I experienced in my younger years growing up here. So, I had my trials and tribulations and I accept people as people. I know I'm a human. We're different cultures, have different skin colors, but day-to-day we're all humans and we are shitty and we're pretty cool, too.

So, I've kept that perspective throughout my life and, you know, I've watched. I stayed in school forever just trying to figure out things. I met a woman that was from Tucson, a Black woman, and we got married and over a few years and we had two great kids. We ended up moving back to Marana where I grew up. And we raised our kids out there in this country, in a white area. But my kids grew up four-wheeling and going out hiking and playing outside, not a lot of city life. They're just the greatest kids now, and they have a great perspective on how they look at the world. Pretty cool.

I have no doubt, though, my friends that I grew up with, that I see on Facebook or just run into, are more conservative. I'm a kind of a moderate politically. But I can see that the bias in some ways that it took me a while to see. This is because when you're young and you're a kid, I think there are less biases, but people age and grow and see the world. So, I see these things. And I always saw, and I felt it was more like it wasn't in your face. It was more like "Hey, how you doing," and then they, you know, are talking shit or I'm more marginalized or excluded in certain ways. I didn't experience [it as an] overwhelming part of my life. I grew up with these white guys and, you know, I played football with them, we acted crazy, and they're still some of my best friends. You know, there was one other Black guy that was an athlete that I went to school with, I consider him my best friend. He's, he's a good guy. So, I have all these those guys that the color of their skin doesn't matter to me and they love me like a brother. And I love them.

I think my experience has been different from people who live in big cities or maybe places where the bias and prejudice is war. I've had encounters with the police here in this town where, like, I think they would have shot somebody in other places. Like, I walked away like not even a ticket. I didn't fear the police that much or be like they were always out to get me or you. I had some good encounters. There was a situation where, like, I could have been on the news or something. And these officers. They were deputies and I was treated fairly, you know, and I know that kills me. You know, I see my 23-year-old son and fear for his life, and I try not to be fearful. Maybe it's an unjust worry but that someone stupid who's not thinking in an unbiased way will do something to hurt my kid, although I've never had that happen, per se. I've had the opposite, like where law enforcement officers have been really cool to me. So, my experience here has been a mixed bag of nuts.

I don't like the word racism. First, A, because it creates the idea that we're from a different race, and I'm not going to go along with that antiquated idea that we're from a different race. Some people walk around being demons, I don't know. So, I'm going to go with A. I'm not going to join that.

Interviews About Early Entertainment in Tucson

Portions of an Interview with Helen Wilkins by Tani Sanchez

We went to movies and house parties. Dances whenever a band would stop here—B.B. King, Lionel Hampton, and Bobby "Blue" Bland and all those big bands. It was either at the Sports Center or the El Camino Ballroom on, I think, South Second. It's a Mexican ballroom, but Blacks rented it. I remember one night that Bobby "Blue" Bland came and he wanted his money in advance and [when they didn't get it] they packed up and left. So, we went by the window and got our money back. T-Bone Walker was forever here because Miss Lilly Walls used to sing with him. Claytie Lokey had a band; she used to sing and play. The dances were for the Blacks but a few whites and Mexicans got in. Mr. Preston and his son had a band but they played mostly for the white clubs.

Ever since I've been in Tucson, I've heard of Juneteenth. I had never heard of it before. They sure used to ask what I was going to do on Juneteenth Day. People use to ask what part of Texas are you from? I'm from Kansas. I didn't know about Juneteenth!

Editor's note: Bobby Bland was a popular singer of the blues performing from the 1950s into the 1980s. Inducted into the Blues Hall of Fame, his music can still be heard on YouTube.

An Essay by Marjorie Hudson Robinson

In 1931, my father, William Hudson, and my mother Willie Mae Haywood Hudson, moved our family from Phoenix to Tucson, where my father had secured a position teaching at Dunbar Junior High School.

The principal was Mr. Lee. Teachers in the elementary section included Mrs. Taylor and Mrs. Nelson (for many years), who were very dedicated and highly respected teachers. A Mrs. Hargrove taught there for a short time in the early thirties. Later, Miss Beatrice Hammonds came to teach us Spanish in the ninth grade.

In the spring of 1934, she coached us girls in basketball. We played by the rather restrictive roles that were used for girls then, though we would have preferred using the freewheeling style of the boys.

Although we were a considerably smaller school and only a junior high, we traveled to play the girls team at Phoenix Senior High, which included the ninth graders (which we were). They beat us soundly, but it was great fun and there was an exciting dance after the game.

During the years at Dunbar, school, home, and church were the hub of our existence. We had parties on Halloween and at Christmastime and dances at the ninth graders' commencement time in late May.

At Easter time the girls would put on frilly pastel dresses and the boys their Sunday best suits and families would go to the programs put on by the Sunday school for the whole church.

One winter morning during the early thirties, we woke up to be greeted by a beautiful white snow-covered desert. And, wonder of wonders, we were given a holiday from school to enjoy a fantasyland we had never expected to see. There was only an inch of snow and it didn't last very long, but it was a great thrill for us.

Sometimes Mr. Hudson would supervise our impromptu baseball and basketball games hastily organized for an hour or so of fun on the playground after school. He ran and played with us. It was wonderful fun. Also, during the spring, he directed plays starring the junior high students. The props and furniture for the plays were loaned by local merchants and the productions were put on at Stafford Junior high auditorium because they had a stage, and we didn't.

One citywide custom during the thirties was the Halloween festival downtown on Congress Street where young goblins, ghosts, witches, and such were all given treats from Donofrio, a local merchant.

Another tradition during the thirties, was the annual "Armistice Day" (now Veterans Day) parade through downtown Tucson. We at Dunbar put on navy blue and gold capes and skirts for the girls and capes with trousers for the boys. After practicing marching for days, on November 11, we paraded. The schools participating were awarded placements for excellence, or lack of it, from the top performance down.

A summer custom that some of us followed was to have a picnic in celebration of the Emancipation Proclamation on June 19th. We children looked forward to it as a day of ball games and delicious food such as ice cream and watermelon. We usually chose the countryside near the San Xavier Del Bac for a large family outing.

In the mid-thirties, Mr. Lee left Dunbar to become principal at the "colored" senior high school in Phoenix. Mr. Perry replaced him for a while. Later Mr. Maxwell became principal at Dunbar.

In connection with church, two people are etched in happy memory: Reverend Hamilton and his wife. They moved from Tanner Chapel A.M.E. Church in Phoenix to Prince Chapel A.M.E. in Tucson. They opened up their hearts and home to us, the youngsters, and frequently supervised socials for us on the spacious lawn at the parsonage. We spent many festive afternoons and evenings enjoying simple pleasures; a little food and a lot of fun and games. They made the parsonage ours. The C.M.E. (Colored Methodist Episcopal Church) and Mount Calvary Baptist Church also made the children welcome at various activities. The

Blacks at Sabino Canyon circa 1940s. Photo from the Marguerite Euell Sanchez collection.

custom during those early years was for most churches to have evening, as well as morning Sunday services.

In the twenties, Wylie Haywood Sr. (from Texas) came to Arizona and became a desert rancher. He bought a somewhat large parcel of land just south of Tucson. He was married to Addie Long, sister of Grover Long, who was also an early resident of Tucson. In addition to his children and hers, the Haywoods had two children together: Wylie Haywood the younger, and Audrey Haywood Smith, now of San Francisco.

Another early resident was Mr. Louis Washington, who was the owner of one of the few "Negro" owned business in early Tucson. He operated a filling station on Main Avenue toward the north side of the city. Washington suffered a traumatic blow when a gasoline truck had an accident on his corner that caused an explosion and a terrible fire which destroyed his station. Mr. Washington married Lorraine, a teacher, who had a son, Franklin McDonald.

Joe Baptiste

Another well-known citizen of Tucson was Dr. Thompson, who was our only Black physician during the 1930s.

Our outstanding sports hero of the thirties was Joe Batiste, who excelled at track. He was a star who ran the hurdles like a god—who simply spread his legs and sailed over, setting national records for speed. It was a never-to-be-forgotten spectacle to watch him.

During those early years, after Arizona became a state in 1912, many Black people moved there from the South, searching to improve their family's circumstances and to seek a good education for their children.

Many came to improve their health because of having contracted tuberculosis or having developed some other condition that the warm, dry Arizona desert could help.

I feel lucky to have been born in Arizona and to have had many happy experiences there.

Postscript: When I started writing these memories there were first names of people who were adults when I was growing up that I couldn't recall for certain. But now I feel sure that Mr. Lee's first name was Roy. Mr. Maxwell's first name was Morgan. However, I'm not sure of Mr. Perry's first name yet. He stayed in Tucson for a much shorter time.

Also, somehow, I forgot to mention how, in the early thirties, we youngsters would walk to the Plaza Theater on the west end of Congress Street, to lay down our nickel

Visiting Oury Park, Left to right top: Roy Stinson, "Pee Wee," Sam Hollis, Bottom, William Swancey, Frank Baptiste, Opal, Maceo Wells.

and see a rousing program of Western movies and breathtaking cliffhanger serials as well as cartoons.

We gave little thought to the fact that we were sitting in the balcony. The other kids were there too! It was more affordable. The balcony was packed.

Marguerite Sanchez collection

And some of my most pleasant memories are of the Girl Reserves and meetings at the YWCA. We had candlelight ceremonies and parties there. Also, we went on hikes to the countryside and camp outs where we fried bacon and eggs over an open fires and roasted marshmallows and hot dogs on a stick. And we sang with the crickets at the top of our voices in the wonderful night air.

Editor's note: Marjorie Hudson was a former Tucson teacher and real estate agent. Born in Nogales, Arizona, she graduated from the University of Arizona. She married Charles Robinson, an airman stationed in Tucson at Davis-Monthan Air Force Base, in 1945. She eventually moved to Baltimore, Maryland and died there.

Recipes: Cakes and Sweet Things

MA'S GLAZED DOUGHNUT
Tina L. Johnson
Yield: about 2 dozen

Ingredients:
For doughnuts:
¾ cup milk
¼ cup sugar
1 teaspoon salt
¼ cup butter
¼ cup warm water
1 packet yeast
1 egg, beaten
3¼ cups sifted flour, divided
Additional flour for dusting
Oil for frying

For glazes or toppings:
2 cups sifted powdered sugar
⅓ cup milk
1 teaspoon vanilla or maple flavoring
Cinnamon (optional)

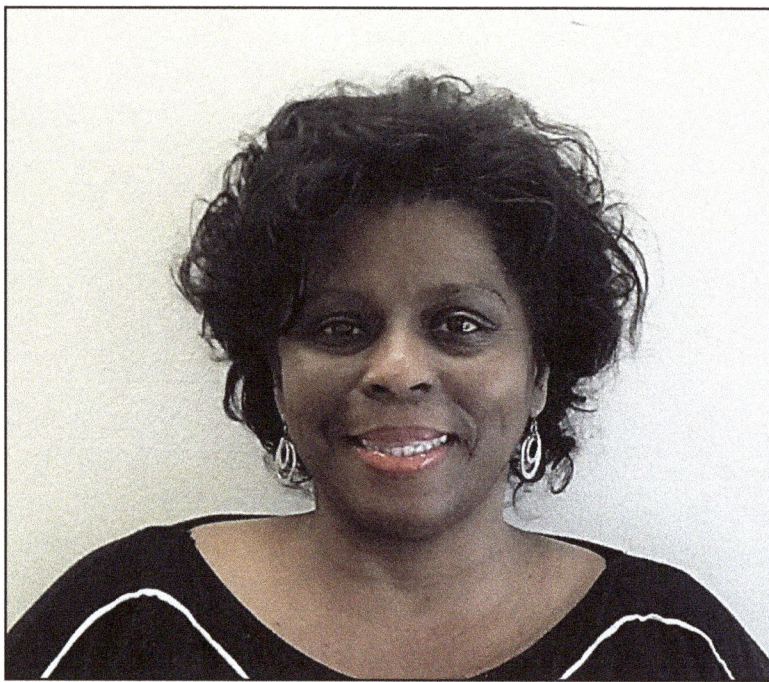

Scald milk over low heat. Stir in sugar, salt, and butter. Set aside.

Measure warm (not hot) water into a warm medium-sized bowl. Add yeast and stir gently until dissolved. Stir in warm milk mixture, egg, and half the flour (about 2 cups). Add remaining flour—about 1¾ cups, or enough to make a soft dough. Turn onto lightly floured board. Knead until smooth and elastic but not stiff. Place in a lightly greased bowl, turning once to grease top. Cover and let rise in a warm place until the dough doubles in size—about an hour.

Punch down dough once to release the air. Roll out on lightly floured board to about ½-inch thick. Cut into shapes or use a 2½-inch round cutter for doughnuts and holes. Separate doughnut holes from doughnuts. Gently place doughnuts onto greased baking sheets, leaving about 1 inch between each doughnut. Cover and let rise about one hour.

Handle doughnuts as little as possible to prevent them from flattening. Fry for 2–3 minutes until light brown on both sides, turning halfway through. Transfer and drain on rack. While still warm, carefully dip in glaze, cinnamon and sugar, or powdered sugar. Drain glazed doughnuts on a wire rack over a board or wax paper to catch drips for reuse. (Occasionally scrape glaze from the board or wax paper into the glaze bowl and stir to recombine.)

Glaze: Combine powdered sugar, milk, and flavoring and stir until smooth.

Tina L. Johnson is a former program Coordinator at the University of Arizona and Development Associate at the Women's Foundation of Southern Arizona. She is currently an administrative assistant at the University of Arizona and serves as a website content manager.

CORN PUDDING
Yvonne Gathers

Ingredients:
1 (15-ounce) can whole kernel corn
½ cup sugar
½ cup milk
2 large eggs
¼ cup butter, melted
½ teaspoon vanilla
Dash salt
Dash pepper
Dash nutmeg
Dash cinnamon

Mix all ingredients and pour into a greased baking dish. Bake at 350°F for about 50 minutes.

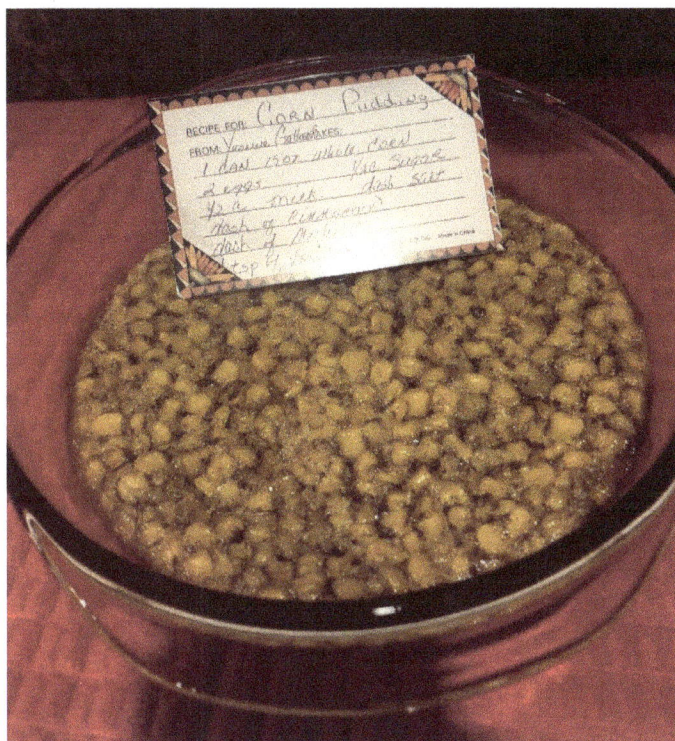

Yvonne Gathers retired in 2010 from the University of Arizona but is currently clinical director and acting administrator for two group homes in Sahuarita. She says, "I have been making a lot of foods healthier in terms of not frying so much. We sometimes do more Asian type dishes, baking … Although I love fried chicken, we are opting to bake it. … We're not eating as much bread. We eat way more vegetables. My husband had a heart attack about four years ago, so that changed his eating habits, and it made us all very conscious of the different foods that we eat and how much."

CORN PUDDING
Felix Goodwin
Felix Goodwin, formerly a Public Affairs Officer at Fort Huachuca, became the assistant to President Harvill for minority affairs at the University of Arizona in 1969. He is credited with attracting numerous African Americans to campus.
Serves 4.

Ingredients:
1 16-ounce can cream-style corn, *or* 2½ cups fresh corn kernels
1 cup whole milk
1 tablespoon cornstarch
1 teaspoon salt
1 teaspoon pepper

3 eggs beaten
2 tablespoons melted butter
1 teaspoon vanilla
½ teaspoon cinnamon
1 tablespoon sugar (or more to taste)

If you are using fresh corn, cook it and then cut the kernels off the cob. Mix all the ingredients together. Stir well. Pour into a ½-quart casserole. Place in a 350°F oven and cook for 45 minutes or until the pudding is set.

LEMON PUDDING
Elgie Batteau

Ingredients:

4 tablespoons butter

2 cups sugar

4 tablespoons flour

4 eggs, separated

2 lemons, juiced, and grated rind

2 cups milk

Cream butter and sugar, add flour, put in eggs yolks, lemon rind and juice. Add cups of milk at intervals.

Beat egg whites stiff but not dry, fold into mixture. Bake in 350°F oven in water until a knife will come out clean when stuck into the middle of pudding.

VEGETARIAN SOUL BUTTERMILK PIE
Monicia Porter

Ingredients:

Crust:

3 cups all-purpose flour

2 teaspoons sugar

½ teaspoon salt

½ cup vegan butter

½ cup vegetable shortening

3 to 5 tablespoons ice water

Filling:

3 eggs

1½ cups granulated sugar

½ cup butter, softened

3 tablespoons all-purpose flour

⅛ teaspoon of salt

1 cup room-temperature vegan buttermilk (*or* 1 cup almond milk mixed with 1 teaspoon of lemon juice)

1 tablespoon lemon juice

1 teaspoon vanilla extract

For crust: Refrigerate your butter and shortening for 1 hour before prep.

In a bowl, whisk or sift together flour, sugar, and salt. Cut the butter and shortening into small cubes and add to the bowl. Use a pastry cutter or fork to cut in the butter and shortening to the flour mixture. The result should look like coarse meal. Drizzle in 2 tablespoons of ice-cold water and mix. Add water 1 tablespoon at a time until dough begins to clump together.

Tip the dough onto a lightly floured surface and, manipulating it as little as possible, shape it into 2 even-sized balls. Roll one ball with a rolling pin into about a circle about 12 inches in diameter and transfer to a pie plate. Gently push the pie crust all around the dish, trimming off any excess and reworking any spots that are thin or need repair. Repeat with remaining dough. Refrigerate until you are ready to use.

For filling: Preheat oven to 375°F. Thoroughly mix eggs, sugar, butter, flour, and salt. Stir in buttermilk, lemon juice, and vanilla until well combined. Pour equal parts into the unbaked pie crusts and bake for 40–45 minutes until a toothpick or fork in the middle comes out clean. Remove from oven and allow to cool at least 20 minutes before serving.

Editor's note: Monicia Porter is school counselor at Tucson High Magnet School. She says the COVID-19 pandemic has inspired her to find new recipes for her husband, who likes sweets. "There are a couple of things that I always baked well that people liked, and that's what I stuck to. But I began to look for recipes … my husband has a sweet tooth. He can afford it, I can't. So, cookies and things that were healthy, healthy substitutions to those. I'm allergic to dairy. Because of that I make my own ice creams with mangos and strawberries and almond milk."

LEMON SQUARES
Murryelle and Frank Bothwell

Frank is retired military veteran who describes himself as "Afrocentric … a 78-year-old senior who thinks he's 20 and I'm proud of my race and I'm excited that you're interviewing us about anything that deals with us as Black people." Murryelle is a retired nurse practitioner and therapist. She calls the recipe a family classic. "It was my mother's favorite. I called sisters I have and when I asked them about my mother's favorite recipe, the first thing that came out of their mouth was lemon squares. And I have shared the recipe with our granddaughter. Two of the granddaughters said the same thing. It's easy to make it, delicious. We all love lemon squares." The Bothwells lived for several months in Ghana, while traveling to African countries. Frank published a book, *Sankofa*, about their experiences. They are active in Black organizations and issues.

Ingredients:
Topping:
2 eggs
1 cup of sugar
½ teaspoon baking powder
¼ teaspoon salt
2 tablespoons lemon juice

confectioners' sugar for dusting

Base:
1 cup of flour
½ cup of butter
¼ cup of confectioners' sugar

Base: Blend flour, butter, and sugar and press into an 8-inch pan. Bake at 350°F for 20 minutes. **Topping:** Beat eggs, adding sugar gradually. Add baking powder, salt, and lemon juice and mix with a mixer. Pour over hot crust, return to oven and bake 20 minutes longer, or until lightly browned. Do not overbake. Dust with confectioners' sugar while still warm.

Photo by Tani Sanchez

Editor's note: The following old-school recipe desert contributions are really good. They are sweet and authentic. If you want to reduce the sugar, as mentioned earlier, try substitutes. Swerve is made from erythritol and is a sugar alcohol. The Mayo Clinic says "sugar alcohols (polyols) are carbohydrates that occur naturally in certain fruits and vegetables—although they can also be manufactured. Despite their name, sugar alcohols aren't alcoholic because they don't contain ethanol, which is found in alcoholic beverages." These sugars don't cause tooth decay, and various types and blends are sold. Monk fruit is a favorite as well. It is made from a plant and may have antioxidant benefits. Allulose or allulose blend sweeteners are often substituted in lemon meringue pies. Swerve is sold online and available at Fry's and other supermarkets. Swerve comes in confectioners' sugar, granular sugar, and brown sugar varieties. I used it as a substitute in the sweet potato pie recipes and they were great. In terms of the sweet potato pies, my twist is to add organic yams along with the organic sweet potatoes for a mixed pie. Secondly, I cook them in an Instant Pot—great for someone who wants to do things easily. Rinse yams and pierce them with a fork. Place them on a trivet in the Instant Pot and cook for about 35 minutes on high pressure. Let them cool a bit, then cut lengthwise and scoop the flesh out with a spoon. I made some sweet potato pies from recipes in this section. To test them, I gave slices to various people around town. They said they were very good. I agreed.

GREAT-GRANDMOTHER'S PECAN PIE
Barbara Tucker

Ingredients:

2 eggs

1 cup sugar

1 cup of Karo light syrup

1 teaspoon butter

1½ teaspoons vanilla

1 cup of pecans

1 pie shell

Mix eggs and sugar together until smooth, then add syrup and butter. Mix until smooth. Add vanilla and then pecans. Pour in the pie shell and bake for one hour on 325°F. Let cool before cutting.

Barbara Tucker was a teenager when she came to Tucson. She loved the area, particularly the mountains and the scenery. The mother of two daughters, Antonetta and Morgan, she is remembered by Morgan as an "amazing mother and friend. She was a caregiver, making sure everyone was taken care of."

GRANDMA'S SWEET POTATO PIE
Beverely Elliott

Ingredients:

4 large sweet potatoes

¼ cup margarine

1½ scoops sugar

½ cup brown sugar, packed

2 eggs, separated

¼ cup milk

1 tablespoon vanilla

¾ teaspoon cinnamon

½ teaspoon salt

¼ teaspoon nutmeg

1 large frozen pie crust, thawed

Boil sweet potatoes in a large pot until a fork penetrates easily. Drain, skin, and beat with a mixer. Remove strings from mixer and discard. Add margarine. Beat. Discard strings. Add sugars and egg yolks; beat. Add milk, vanilla, cinnamon, salt, and nutmeg; beat. Remove strings. Add egg whites and beat until fluffy. Prick thawed crust 6 or 7 times. Bake at 350°F for 5 minutes. Remove and let crust cool 2 minutes, then add pie filling. Bake at 350°F for 35–40 minutes or until filling is solid.

Editor's note: I am not sure what a scoop is. I used about ¾ cup sweetener. Adjust for your own taste.

GREAT-GRANDMOTHER'S SWEET POTATO PIE
Barbara Tucker
Ingredients:

2 cups mashed sweet potatoes

½ stick butter, softened

1 small (6 ounce) can of Pet evaporated milk

1¼ cup of sugar

3 to 4 teaspoons of vanilla

½ teaspoon nutmeg

2 eggs, slightly beaten

1 pie crust

Mix sweet potatoes, softened butter, milk, and sugar until smooth. Add vanilla and nutmeg. Mix, then add eggs (always add eggs last). Mix, pour into pie shell and bake at 325°F for 45 minutes. Remove and let cool before cutting.

LEMON MERINGUE PIE
Anonymous 1993

Ingredients:

½ cup of sugar

1 envelope unflavored gelatin

⅔ cup water

4 eggs, separated

⅓ cup lemon juice

1 tablespoon grated lemon peel

2 teaspoons cream of tartar

9 inch pie crust

½ tablespoon sugar

Put sugar in a double boiler. Add gelatin, water, egg yolks, lemon juice, lemon peel, and cream of tartar. Cook over medium heat until firm. Let cool by placing top of double boiler in a bowl of cool water.

Bake pie crust. Pour cool filling into baked crust. Whip egg whites until stiff. Add ½ tablespoon sugar and a pinch of cream of tartar. Spread over pie. Bake in top of oven until egg whites are brown.

BAKED CHERRY CHEESE PIE
Jazena Hopkins

Ingredients:

8 ounces cream cheese

1 can Eagle Brand sweetened condensed milk

1 teaspoon vanilla

1 teaspoon lemon juice

½ can cherry pie filling

Cream cheese until soft and fluffy. Add Eagle Brand milk, vanilla, and lemon juice. Mix and pour into 9-inch pie crust. Top with cherry pie filling. Bake at 375°F about 20 minutes or until crust is brown.

PEACH COBBLER
Anonymous 1993

Ingredients:

2 large cans peaches

2 cups sugar

1 stick butter, softened

3 tablespoons flour

½ tablespoon nutmeg

½ tablespoon cinnamon

Pie crust

Mix first 6 ingredients together. Place pie crust in a 13" × 9" × 2" pan. Put peach mixture in pan and use extra pie crust dough to make decorative strips on top. Cook in middle of oven for 1 to 1½ hours at 325°F or until it bubbles on top.

DALE'S PECAN PIE
Marguerite Euell Sanchez

Ingredients:

3 whole eggs

1 cup sugar

½ cup syrup

1 stick margarine

1 teaspoon vanilla flavor

1 cup chopped pecans

Mix the above ingredients. Pour into a prepared pie crust. Bake at 325°F for 45 minutes to 1 hour.

BEAN PIE
Chef W. Rutledge White, Submitted by Lorraine White

Ingredients:

2 cups of dried beans (pinto, limas, etc.)

3 eggs

5⅓ ounces evaporated milk

¼ cup cold milk

1 cup sugar

1 teaspoon cinnamon

1 teaspoon ground ginger

½ teaspoon ground nutmeg

¼ teaspoon cloves

1 tablespoon vegetable oil

½ teaspoon salt

9 inch pie shell

Whipped cream

Soak beans in about 3 cups water. Do not discard water.

Beat eggs until frothy, add both milks; stir until smooth. Add sugar and spices, mix, and turn into pie shell.

Puree soaked beans. Add 1 cup pureed beans, and 2½ cups of the soaking water to the pie mix, along with salt and vegetable oil. Bake in 375°F oven for 1 hour.

SWEET POTATO PONE
B. Lucille Lewis, submitted for her mother Louise Warner
Serves 6.

Ingredients:

½ cup sugar

½ cup butter

½ cup milk

2 cups grated, uncooked sweet potatoes

1 teaspoon allspice

½ teaspoon nutmeg

½ teaspoon salt

¼ teaspoon cinnamon

Blend sugar and butter and add milk and sweet potatoes. Beat well. Blend in salt and spices. Place in shallow buttered pan. Bake at 325°F for 1 hour.

MRS. EUELL'S BROWNIES
Mrs. Marguerite Euell Sanchez
Ingredients:

½ pound butter

1 pound margarine or Crisco

2½ cup sugar

4 squares chocolate, melted

4 eggs

1½ cup flour

2 teaspoons vanilla

1½ cup walnuts and pecans

Preheat oven to 300°F.

Cream butter, sugar, and margarine. Add cooled chocolate. Add eggs, one at a time. Beat well after each egg. Add flour, vanilla, and nuts. Pour mix into greased 13" × 9" cake pan. Bake 25–30 minutes. Cut when cool.

CHEESE COOKIES
Hearon Hayes
Yield: about 8 dozen.

Ingredients:

2 cups cheddar cheese, grated

1 cup soft butter

2 cups shifted flour

1 teaspoon salt

Cream the cheese and butter together. Add flour and salt and mix until dough is smooth and well blended. Shape dough into rolls, about an inch in diameter. Chill 2 hours until dough is firm. Preheat oven to 350°F. Slice the dough into thin rounds. Place on ungreased baking sheets at least an inch apart. Bake 12–15 minutes.

PRUNE WHIP
Mrs. Lola Brownlow
This recipe was brought with Mrs. Brownlow from Little Rock, Arkansas. It was used by her as a light dessert for her guests. Her husband was Mr. James Brownlow of the 371st Regiment, 92nd Infantry Division at Fort Huachuca. He was Tucson's first African American disc jockey.

Ingredients:

3 egg whites, beaten until stiff

½ cup powdered confectioners' sugar

1 cup of stewed, pitted, chopped prunes

Gradually fold sugar into egg whites. Fold prunes into mixture until light. Place in a buttered baking dish. Bake in 350°F oven for 15 minutes. Serve. Can serve when warm with a soft custard (that you may have made from the leftover egg yolks) or with whipped cream.

SUGAR COOKIES
Elgie Batteau

Ingredients:

2 cups flour
½ teaspoon salt
2 teaspoons baking powder
1 cup shortening

1 cup sugar
2 eggs
2 or more teaspoons flavoring, vanilla or lemon

Sift flour, salt, and baking powder together. Cream shortening and sugar. Add eggs, beat well. Mix in flavoring. Gradually add sifted ingredients to creamed mixture. Shape into balls, about 1 teaspoon each. Space on greased cookie sheet. Flatten with a flat-bottom glass greased and dipped in sugar. Bake at 375°F until brown.

Editor's note: You can substitute superfine blanched almond flour blended with ⅓ cup coconut flour and add extra shortening or eggs. Also, you can use a monk fruit sweetener.

BETTER THAN SEX CAKE
Helen Wilkins

Ingredients:

1 (18½ ounce) box yellow cake mix
1 (20 ounce) can crushed pineapple
2 to 3 packages instant vanilla pudding
3 cups milk
1 cup whipping cream

¾ cup granulated sugar
¼ cup powdered sugar
1 teaspoon vanilla
½ cup shredded coconut, toasted in 350°F
preheated oven, watched carefully

Prepare cake mix per directions on box. Pour batter into a 9″ × 13″ cake pan, spread evenly. Bake at 350°F for 30 to 35 minutes. Remove from oven. Cool in pan for 5–10 minutes. With a fork, punch holes in warm cake at 1″ intervals. Spread crushed pineapple over the cake. Cool completely.

Make up pudding with the milk. Beat with a wire whip until thick. Spread over cooled cake. Refrigerate for a few hours or overnight.

Shortly before serving time, make whipped cream (whip together whipping cream, granulated sugar, powdered sugar, and vanilla) and spread over the refrigerated cake. Top with toasted coconut. Serve cool.

POUND CAKE
Jazena Hopkins

Ingredients:
1 pound butter, soft
10 eggs, separated at room temperature
1 teaspoon vanilla
2 cups sugar, divided
3 cups cake flour (or use 2 tablespoons cornstarch per cup of all-purpose flour)
1 teaspoon baking powder

Combine butter, egg yolks, 1½ cups sugar and vanilla. Beat 5 minutes until creamy. Add flour and baking powder slowly until thoroughly mixed. In a separate bowl, beat egg whites until light. Add remaining ½ cup sugar. Beat until stiff. Fold into batter. Bake at 350°F for 1 hour. Cool on rack.

Editor's note: To make a glaze for this cake, mix 2-3 or more cups of powdered sugar with milk or lemon. The powdered sugar will absorb the liquid very quickly so add this slowly and by teaspoons. The mixture should pour easily but not be runny. Drizzle over the cooled cake.

My grandmother and many of her era made pound cakes that were extraordinarily memorable. I have tried making them using a low carb flour substitute but they all came up short. Some were sort of okay with blends of coconut flour, but none compared to the older recipes. Pound cakes can be sprinkled with confectioners' sugar, icing or a glaze and served with fruits such as strawberries or raspberries. Purists will argue that a true pound cake has no baking powder, but this recipe is worth trying.

Name Index

Recipe Index

Partial List of Sources

African American Student Affairs. 2020. "Welcome to AASA!" Accessed December 7, 2019. https://aasa.arizona.edu/.

———. 2020. "Building Leaders and Creating Knowledge (B.L.A.C.K.)." Accessed July 28, 2020. https://aasa.arizona.edu/building-leaders-and-creating-knowledge.

University of Arizona, "Unit History," Africana Studies Academic Program Review Self-Study Report 2013. Tucson, Arizona.

American Heart Association. 2018. "Carbohydrates." Healthy Living. Last updated April 16, 2018. www.heart.org/en/healthy-living/healthy-eating/eat-smart/nutrition-basics/carbohydrates.

Arizona Historical Society. Mary Wright Euell Collection of minutes and other documents of the Women's Progressive and Civic Club, 1930s through 1970s, uncatalogued. Tucson, Arizona.

Associated Press, KVOA, and 12 News. 2019. "Accused Students Identified in Racist Attack on Black Student at University of Arizona." KVUE.com. Published September 13, 2019. https://www.kvue.com/article/news/local/arizona/university-of-arizona-hate-crime-under-investigation/75-c87e72ee-4eef-496d-acbc-84586ac80e3d.

Bower, A. L. 2008. *African American Foodways: Explorations of History and Culture*. Champaign, IL: University of Illinois Press.

Centers for Disease Control. 2021. "Preparing Chitlins Safely." Last reviewed October 18, 2021. www.cdc.gov/foodsafety/communication/chitlins.html.

Cherniwchan, J., and J. Moreno-Cruz. 2018. "Maize and Precolonial Africa." *Journal of Development Economics* 136 (January 2019): 137–50. Published online October 30, 2018. https://doi.org/10.1016/j.jdeveco.2018.10.008.

Collins, K. 2016. "Which Is Healthier, a Tortilla or a Slice of Bread?" American Institute for Cancer Research. Published June 13, 2016. www.aicr.org/resources/blog/health-talk-which-is-healthier-a-tortilla-or-a-slice-of-bread/.

Daniels, R. (2020, August 16). The Red, Black & Green: Fly the flag and fight for the exoneration of Marcus Garvey. Institute of the Black World 21st Century. Retrieved February 19, 2022, from https://ibw21.org/commentary/vantage-point-articles/the-red-black-and-green-fly-the-flag-and-fight-for-the-exoneration-of-marcus-garvey/

Donella, Leah. 2017. "On Flag Day, Remembering The Red, Black And Green." NPR, June 14, 2017. https://www.npr.org/sections/codeswitch/2017/06/14/532667081/on-flag-day-remembering-the-red-black-and-green#:~:text=The%20Pan%2DAfrican%20flag's%20colors,the%20natural%20fertility%20of%20Africa.

Eppinga, J. Henry O. Flipper in the Court of Private Land Claims: The Arizona career of West Point's first Black graduate. Through Our Parents' Eyes. Retrieved February 17, 2022, from https://parentseyes.arizona.edu/content/1244.

———. "Long Live Flipper." Retrieved February 22, 2022, from http://trendmag2.trendoffset.com/publication/?i=409912&article_id=2790316&view=articleBrowser.

Fernandez, M. 2018. "Tucson Race Riot (1967)." BlackPast.org. Published March 25, 2018. www.blackpast.org/african-american-history/tucson-race-riot-1967/.

Fodor's Travels. "Why would the Holy Office of the Inquisition care about a bread pudding recipe?" Retrieved February 19, 2022. https://www.fodors.com/world/mexico-and-central-america/mexico/experiences/news/there-are-a-lot-of-wild-legends-about-mexicos-iconic-easter-dish-heres-the-truth.

Fort Davis National Historic Site, National Park Service. "Second Lieutenant Henry O. Flipper: First Black Graduate of West Point." Retrieved February 19, 2022. http://npshistory.com/brochures/foda/flipper.pdf.

Garcia, J. 2013, March 4. Black soldiers in the Revolutionary War. www.army.mil. Retrieved February 19, 2022, from https://www.army.mil/article/97705/black_soldiers_in_the_revolutionary_war

Harvard Medical School. 2014. "Is a Vegetarian or Vegan Diet for You?" Staying Healthy. Published April 12, 2014. www.health.harvard.edu/staying-healthy/is-a-vegetarian-or-vegan-diet-for-you.

Harvard School of Public Health. 2019. "Fish: Friend or Foe?" The Nutrition Source. Published May 22, 2019. www.hsph.harvard.edu/nutritionsource/fish/.

Keith L. 2011. "The Redevelopment of the Ghost Ranch Lodge." https://www.laddkeith.com/106/the-redevelopment-of-the-ghost-ranch-lodge/

Kestenbaum, D. (2012, November 15). Why Coke cost a nickel for 70 years. NPR. Retrieved June 18, 2022, from https://www.npr.org/sections/money/2012/11/15/165143816/why-coke-cost-a-nickel-for-70-years

Lachman, R. 2020. "Is Uncured Bacon Healthier or Hype?" Published December 29, 2020. Health Essentials. Cleveland Clinic. https://health.clevelandclinic.org/uncured-bacon-healthier-or-hype/.

Lawson, H. *1991 -- African American settlers in Tucson.* 1991 -- African American Settlers in Tucson | Through Our Parents' Eyes. Retrieved February 21, 2022, from https://parentseyes.arizona.edu/node/40

Mayo Clinic Staff. 2020. "Artificial Sweeteners and Other Sugar Substitutes." Healthy Lifestyle. Mayo Clinic. Published October 8, 2020. www.mayoclinic.org/healthy-lifestyle/nutrition-and-healthy-eating/in-depth/artificial-sweeteners/art-20046936.

Migoya, C. 2021. "This Tucson Teen Is on a Crusade to Require Anti-Racist Lessons at School." *Arizona Daily Star*, updated May 10, 2021. https://tucson.com/news/local/this-tucson-teen-is-on-a-crusade-to-require-anti-racist-lessons-at-school/article_f79e460a-b214-5283-802f-c417be2bb620.html.

National Park Service. "WEBINAR: Buffalo Soldiers in Parks| A Case Study." Retrieved February 19, 2022. https://www.nps.gov/subjects/civilrights/webinar-buffalo-soldiers-in-parks-a-case-study.htm#:~:text=American%20Plains%20Indians%20who%20fought,with%20all%20African%2DAmerican%20regiments.

New York Times. 1992. "Campus Police Attend Classes on Sensitivity." February 16, 1992.
www.nytimes.com/1992/02/16/nyregion/campus-life-arizona-campus-police-attend-classes-on-sensitivity.html.

Notice of regular governing board meeting Tucson, AZ 85709 ... - pima.edu. Pima County Community
College District Governing Board Open Meeting Notice and Agenda October 11, 2017. (n.d.).
Retrieved October 23, 2021, from https://www.pima.edu/about-pima/leadership-policies/governing-board/board-meetings/packets-2015-18/201710-bogpacket-all.pdf

Olsson, R. 2020. "Is Monk Fruit a Healthy Sugar Alternative?" Banner Health.
www.bannerhealth.com/healthcareblog/teach-me/is-monk-fruit-a-healthy-sugar-alternative.

Pima County School Superintendent's Office. 2022. "14th Annual Autism Walk & Resource Fair."
http://www.schools.pima.gov/14th-annual-autism-walk-resource-fair.

Procida, M.A. 2003. Feeding the Imperial Appetite: Imperial Knowledge and Anglo-Indian Discourse.
Journal of Women's History 15(2), 123-149. doi:10.1353/jowh.2003.0054.

Prendergast, C. 2020. "Hundreds Attend Peaceful, yet Forceful, Tucson Vigil a Week after Killing of
George Floyd." *Arizona Daily Star*, updated June 30, 2020.
https://tucson.com/news/local/hundreds-attend-peaceful-yet-forceful-tucson-vigil-a-week-after-killing-of-george-floyd/article_912ad07c-a484-11ea-bd2c-07b219370a18.html.

Serrato, L. 2021. "Med Schools Eye Change as States Declare Racism a Public Health Threat." Cronkite
News. *Arizona Daily Star*, updated April 30, 2021. https://tucson.com/news/arizona_news/med-schools-eye-change-as-states-declare-racism-a-public-health-threat/article_4dd8a2bf-8720-5196-ad68-8b7be86f103e.html.

Smith, S. L. 1995. *Sick and Tired of Being Sick and Tired: Black Women's Health Activism in America,
1890–1950*. Philadelphia: University of Pennsylvania Press.

Soul Origin. N.d. Accessed December 7, 2019. https://www.soulorigin.com.au/blog-mulligatawnysoup/.

Swedlund, E. 2007. "Blackface Party Reveals Ignorance, Racism, UA Students Say." *Arizona Daily Star*,
February 16, 2007. https://tucson.com/news/blackface-party-reveals-ignorance-racism-ua-students-say/article_d270a0d3-be2e-522b-b643-dd2aa9432e7f.html.

Tucson.com. 2022. "Photos: The Old Pueblo Club on the 21st floor above Tucson in 1966."
https://tucson.com/news/retrotucson/photos-the-old-pueblo-club-on-the-st-floor-above/collection_c30c521a-3677-11e7-b09c-7354085418e5.html#1.

Tucson Black Film. 2015. "First Annual Film Festival." https://tucsonbfc.weebly.com/

U.S. Army Environmental Command. 2014. *Supplemental Programmatic Environmental Assessment for
Army 2020 Force Structure Realignment*. June 2014.
https://aec.army.mil/application/files/9414/9520/0012/Army2020SPEA-3.pdf.

U.S. Census Bureau quickfacts: Tucson City, Arizona. (n.d.). Retrieved February 17, 2022, from
https://www.census.gov/quickfacts/tucsoncityarizona

U.S. Department of the Interior. (n.d.). Second lieutenant Henry Flipper. National Parks Service. Retrieved February 17, 2022, from https://www.nps.gov/foda/learn/historyculture/secondlieutenanthenryflipper.htm

U.S. Department of Agriculture. n.d. "Make Half Your Grains Whole Grains." MyPlate. www.myplate.gov/eat-healthy/grains.

U.S. Food and Drug Administration. 2017. "High-Intensity Sweeteners." Last updated December 19, 2017. www.fda.gov/food/food-additives-petitions/high-intensity-sweeteners.

West, C. 2003. Prophesy deliverance!: An Afro-American revolutionary Christianity. Westminster John Knox Press.

———. 2018. Race matters. Beacon Press.

Wallach, J. J. 2015. *Dethroning the Deceitful Pork Chop: Rethinking African American Foodways from Slavery to Obama*. Fayetteville: University of Arkansas Press.

Williams, R. 1986. *They Stole It, but You Must Return It*. [US]: HEMA Publishing.

Yancy, J. W. (1933). *The Negro of Tucson, Past and Present*. [Master's thesis, University of Arizona].

Zeldovich, L. 2018. "14,000-Year-Old Piece of Bread Rewrites the History of Baking and Farming." NPR, July 24, 2018. https://www.npr.org/sections/thesalt/2018/07/24/631583427/14-000-year-old-piece-of-bread-rewrites-the-history-of-baking-and-farming.

Additional Information Resources

Alkon, A. H., and J. Agyeman, eds. 2011. *Cultivating Food Justice: Race, Class, and Sustainability*. Cambridge, MA: MIT Press.

Anthony Ryan Hatch. Blood Sugar. Minneapolis: University of Minnesota Press, 2016.

Bailey, Z. D., N. Krieger, M. Agénor, J. Graves, N. Linos, and M. T. Bassett. 2017. "Structural Racism and Health Inequities in the USA: Evidence and Interventions." *Lancet* 389 (10077): 1453–63.

Carney, J. A., and R. N. Rosomoff. 2011. *In the Shadow of Slavery: Africa's Botanical Legacy in the Atlantic World*. Berkeley: University of California Press.

Garth, H., and A. M. Reese, eds. 2020. *Black Food Matters: Racial Justice in the Wake of Food Justice*. Minneapolis: University of Minnesota Press.

Harris, Jessica B. 2013. High on the Hog: a Culinary Journey from Africa to America. New York: St Martins Press.

Marin, N., ed. 2020. *Black Imagination: Black Voices on Black Futures*. San Francisco: McSweeney's.

Opie, Frederick Douglass. Hog & Hominy Soul Food from Africa to America. Arts and Traditions of the Table. New York: Columbia University Press, 2008.

Penniman, L. 2018. *Farming While Black: Soul Fire Farm's Practical Guide to Liberation on the Land*. White River Junction, VT: Chelsea Green.

Reese, A. M. 2019. *Black Food Geographies: Race, Self-Reliance, and Food Access in Washington, D.C.* Chapel Hill: University of North Carolina Press.

Travis A Weisse, "Alone in a Sea of Rib-Tips": Alvenia Fulton, Natural Health, and the Politics of Soul Food, Journal of the History of Medicine and Allied Sciences, Volume 74, Issue 3, July 2019, Pages 292–315, https://doi.org/10.1093/jhmas/jrz028

Twitty, Michael. The Cooking Gene: A Journey through African American Culinary History in the Old South. First ed. 2017.

Wallach, Jennifer Jensen, Psyche A. Williams-Forson, and Rebecca Sharpless. 2015. Dethroning the deceitful pork chop: rethinking African American foodways from slavery to Obama. http://site.ebrary.com/id/11081552.

Wallach, Jennifer Jensen. Getting What We Need Ourselves: How Food Has Shaped African American Life. 2019.

White, M. M. 2019. *Freedom Farmers: Agricultural Resistance and the Black Freedom Movement*. Chapel Hill: University of North Carolina Press.

Wilkerson, I. (2021). Caste: The origins of our discontents. Thorndike Press, a part of Gale, a Cengage Company.

Williams, D. R., J. A. Lawrence, and B. A. Davis. 2019. "Racism and Health: Evidence and Needed Research." *Annual Review of Public Health* 40 (2019): 105–25.

National Organizations and Podcasts

Organizations:

Black Church Food Security Network

Black Dirt Farm Collective

Black Urban Growers

Cooperative Food Empowerment Directive

Food Chain Workers Alliance

HEAL Food Alliance

National Black Farmers Association

National Black Food and Justice Alliance

Podcasts:

"Intersectionality Matters" (African American Policy Forum)

The Stoop

Zora's Daughters

Image Credits

Many images are from the recipe contributors who were asked to take pictures of their foods or provide images of themselves.

Others are purchased stock images from Dreamstime Images.

Several historical images were purchased from the Arizona Historical Society; others come from the Sanchez family's private collections or from chapter members such as Effie Gregory.

Tucson Black Film Club images are courtesy of the Tucson Black Film Club. I took images of various Tucson Buildings, of Enid Moore-Cranshaw, of the cornbread slice, of the yams sold in a store and used screenshots of Christ Kingdom Fellowship Church during a Zoom worship service and fellowship.

The Barbea Williams image is used with her permission.

About the author...

Tani D. Sanchez is interested in racial representations in the media and in the study of African American history and culture. She has worked as a newspaper editor, radio news host, and as a media information specialist. An Army veteran, she hosted a news program in Korea and worked in public affairs. Dr. Sanchez is also the first president of the Tucson Chapter Afro-American Historical and Genealogical Society. Her doctorate is in Comparative Literary and Cultural Studies; her master's degree focuses on visual culture/cinema/art history.

www.ingramcontent.com/pod-product-compliance
Lightning Source LLC
Chambersburg PA
CBHW040300100426
42811CB00011B/1324

9 780998 320564